EVERYTHING

ELVIS

FANTASTIC FACTS ABOUT THE KING

BY
HELEN CLUTTON

First published in 2004 by
Virgin Books Ltd
Thames Wharf Studios
Rainville Road
London
W6 9HA

A catalogue record for this book is available from
the British Library.

ISBN 0 7535 0960 1

Designed by Undertow Design
Typeset by Phoenix Photosetting, Lordswood,
Chatham, Kent
Printed and bound in Great Britain by
Bookmarque Ltd, Croydon, Surrey

To David
(my big hunk o' love)
to Christopher and Jonathan
(my little hunks o' love)
and to Sarah Sienesi
(because her name belongs in an Elvis book)

Contents

I want you, I need you, I love you: the year mentioned with each song is the year of recording, not necessarily of release. The album title given is the original album if that is still readily available; otherwise it's a recommended, easily available album. Given Elvis's ouput, many great songs have had to be omitted from the essentials list – for which, many apologies.

I WAS BORN ABOUT 10,000 YEARS AGO

Even global superstars have to start somewhere, and Elvis's beginnings were about as humble as they could be.

Elvis Aron Presley was born at 4.35 a.m. on Tuesday 8 January 1935, to Vernon Elvis and Gladys Love (née Smith) Presley.

His older twin brother, Jesse Garon, was stillborn and was buried the next day in an unmarked grave in the Priceville Cemetery near Tupelo. As a boy Elvis often visited the grave, intrigued perhaps by Gladys's belief that when one twin died, the one that lived gained all the strength of both.

His middle name is spelt 'Aron' on his birth certificate, although Vernon wrote it 'Aaron' on Elvis's grave.

'Elvis' is thought to come from the Norse 'Alwiss', meaning 'all wise'.

Elvis's origins in the Old World are widely disputed, with claims from places as diverse as Ireland, Germany and the Preseli hills in Wales. Recent research suggests that he may in fact have roots in the village of Lonmay in Scotland.

On Elvis's birth certificate Vernon states his profession as labourer, while Gladys is described as a factory worker. The doctor who attended the birth, W.R. Hunt, had his $15 fee paid by welfare.

Elvis was born in the tiny two-room house his father built on Old Saltillo Road in Tupelo, Mississippi. It was a 'shotgun shack' – fire a shotgun from the front door through to the back and you'd hit every room in the house.

Vernon's parents, Minnie Mae and Jesse, lived next door. After her divorce from Jesse in 1947, Minnie Mae came to live with Elvis's family and was to stay with Elvis ever after.

Elvis was blood type O.

Elvis's great-great-great-grandmother on his mother's side was a Cherokee Indian called Morning Dove White. Elvis reckoned that's who he got his cheekbones from.

Elvis's paternal great-great-grandfather was Dunnan Pressley Jr, an army deserter who had three wives on the go at the same time. His daughter Roselle, who dropped one 's' from her surname along the way, never married but nonetheless had nine children, one of whom was Jesse, Vernon's father.

Life revolved around the church, specifically the First Assembly of God church, just around the corner. Two-year-old Elvis would climb off his mother's lap in an attempt to get up to the front and join in with the choir.

In 1938 Vernon was sent to the Mississippi State Penitentiary at Parchman. He'd sold a hog to his employer, Orville Bean, and altered Bean's cheque from four dollars to forty. For months, Elvis only saw his father on prison visits. It was during this time that Gladys and Elvis developed their incredibly close and inter-dependent relationship.

Vernon's imprisonment meant that Gladys was unable to keep up the repayments on their house, so she and Elvis moved in with relatives. They would never return to Old Saltillo Road. Thus began a series of moves around the area over the next few years, as Vernon found and lost a number of labouring jobs.

As a child, Elvis's favourite superhero was Captain Marvel Jr. This character had a lightning bolt logo that Elvis would later take as his own.

Elvis made his first public performance at the age of ten, in the children's talent contest at the Mississippi–Alabama Fair and Dairy Show. He stood on a chair and sang 'Old Shep' without accompaniment. He came fifth.

Elvis's first school was the East Tupelo Consolidated School on Lake Street.

Elvis wanted a bicycle for his eleventh birthday but Gladys was worried that he'd get run over. Plus, a guitar was cheaper, so she got him a guitar instead.

Elvis was a habitual sleepwalker as a child, and once nearly fell out of a window. He remained afraid of sleepwalking throughout his life, and rarely slept alone.

At Milam Junior High School, Elvis was something of a loner, but on his sixth-grade report card he gained top marks for courtesy, reliability, co-operation and industry. He scored 'A's in music, PE and spelling, but only managed 'D's in arithmetic and geography.

Elvis was the only child in his sixth-grade class photo to be wearing overalls, the uniform of the destitute.

In November 1948, when Elvis was thirteen, the Presleys moved to Memphis, Tennessee, in search of a brighter future. As Elvis later said, 'We were broke, man, broke.' They found a home, first at 370 Washington Street, then at 572 Poplar Avenue, a boarding house where they shared a bathroom with three other families and cooked their meals on a hotplate.

A worker from the Memphis Housing Authority inspected where they lived and concluded: 'No privacy ... Need housing ... They seem very nice and deserving.' She put them forward for Lauderdale Courts.

Lauderdale Courts was a public housing project with a rent of $35 a month. In September 1949 the Presleys moved into apartment 328 at 185 Winchester Avenue. Elvis liked living there, and used to practise his guitar in the laundry room.

From 1949 Elvis attended Humes High School in Memphis. He became a cadet in the Reserve Officers Training Corps, was a library volunteer worker, and took up woodwork.

Elvis was issued with his Social Security card in September 1950. His number was 409-52-2002.

In the autumn of 1950 Elvis started work as an usher at Loew's State movie theatre on South Main Street. A girl selling sweets at the theatre gave Elvis a candy bar and a jealous colleague told the boss that Elvis had stolen it. Elvis punched his co-worker, and was promptly fired. When *Jailhouse Rock* premiered at Loew's State six years later, the same boss told Elvis he could have his old job back any time.

In 1952 Elvis briefly got a job at MARL Metal Company, but he was so tired all the time that his schoolwork suffered and Gladys made him quit.

When Gladys got work at St Joseph's Hospital, the family income went above the ceiling for assisted housing so they had to leave Lauderdale Courts. They moved to 698 Saffarans Avenue on the day before Elvis's eighteenth birthday and, although they were only there for three months, that's the address on Elvis's draft card.

In April 1953 Elvis entered the Humes High School annual Minstrel Show. He was the sixteenth-listed act on the bill, described as 'Guitarist – Elvis Prestly [*sic*]'.

The Presleys moved to 462 Alabama Avenue in the spring of 1953. They lived in the downstairs apartment and a rabbi and his family lived upstairs. There was only one bedroom so Elvis slept either with his parents or on the sofa.

Vernon was a passive man with no ambition, and from a young age Elvis was, to all intents and purposes, the head of the house. Early girlfriend Dixie Locke noticed that Elvis seemed to take the role of the father, and his dad that of the little boy.

Elvis graduated from Humes on 3 June 1953, becoming the first member of his family ever to complete high school.

That same year, he hitchhiked over 200 miles to Meridian, Mississippi to enter a country music talent contest. He came second.

FROM A JACK TO A KING

It took just two-and-a-half years for a school leaver to become a superstar. Here's how.

On leaving school in 1953, Elvis went straight to the employment office and got two months' work on the assembly line at MB Parker Machinists' Shop. He then went on to Precision Tool, where he was making artillery shells.

Elvis first went into a recording studio in the summer of 1953, to make a record as a present for his mother. The studio was the Memphis Recording Service (later changed to Sun Studio) and Sun was the name of the record company. The studio had an ad in the phone directory: 'We make records on discs – tape or wire. Personal and commercial recordings. Fine equipment – modern studios.'

When office manager Marion Keisker asked him what kind of singer he was, Elvis said, 'I sing all kinds.' Keisker asked him who he sounded like. 'I don't sound like nobody,' came the reply. Elvis paid four dollars to record 'My Happiness' and 'That's When Your Heartaches Begin'. After he left, Marion Keisker made a note of his name with the comment, 'Good ballad singer. Hold.'

Elvis returned to Sun Studio in January 1954 to do another recording, 'I'll Never Stand In Your Way' and 'It Wouldn't Be The Same Without You'. He went to the studio often, just to hang around, or to ask Marion Keisker if any bands were looking for a singer.

In April 1954 Elvis got a job as a truck driver for $40 a week. He was employed by Crown Electric Company to deliver goods to the electricians. Mrs Harris in the employment office had advised Crown Electric's bosses not to be put off by Elvis's appearance. Elvis remained at Crown Electric for six months.

In the spring of 1954, Elvis went to a tryout for a singer at the Hi Hat club in Memphis. After hearing a couple of Elvis's songs, bandleader Eddie Bond told him to stick to truck driving. Elvis later told a friend, 'That sonofabitch broke my heart.'

On 26 June Sam Phillips, the manager of Sun Studio, was looking for a singer and asked Marion Keisker to call in 'the kid with the sideburns'. Keisker rang Elvis and asked if he could be there by three. Elvis later recalled, 'I was there by the time she hung up the phone.'

'Elvis was probably as nervous as anybody, black or white, that I had seen in front of a microphone,' Sam Phillips was to comment. The singing didn't go quite right that day, but Phillips still felt there was *something*. He decided to put Elvis together with guitarist Scotty Moore and bass player Bill Black from the Starlite Wranglers, a hillbilly band.

Their first rehearsal session was booked for 5 July 1954. The session wasn't going too well so Phillips called a break. As the guys were sitting round sipping Cokes, Elvis started messing around with an old Arthur Crudup song, 'That's All Right'. Phillips knew then he had found what he was looking for. He would later say that the song had been delivered to him on a silver platter.

Two days later, on 7 July 1954, Dewey Phillips played 'That's All Right' on air for the first time. The WHBQ DJ (no relation to Sam Phillips) played it on his *Red, Hot And Blue* evening show. Callers jammed the lines asking for it again, and Phillips played it fourteen times during the one show.

A nervous Elvis was hiding out in the Suzore No 2 cinema in Memphis while the radio show was on. Dewey Phillips phoned Elvis's home asking for him, so Vernon and Gladys went to the cinema and dragged him to the radio station.

Elvis was so scared at the thought of being interviewed that Phillips simply didn't tell him that the microphone was already on. One of the questions he asked was which high school Elvis went to – a polite way of letting the audience know what colour Elvis was. At the end of the chat Elvis said, 'Aren't you going to interview me?' Phillips told him he just had, and Elvis broke out in a cold sweat.

Bob Neal, a DJ at WMPS Radio, was Elvis's first manager. He signed with Elvis at the start of 1955, but he was no match for Tom Parker and he caved in to the Colonel in August.

With Elvis selling records, the Presleys were able to move up the housing ladder. In early 1955 they moved to 2414 Lamar Avenue, a small rented house but, crucially, the first building in Memphis that they had all to themselves. After six months they moved again, to 1414 Getwell Road – the house from which Elvis would sign with RCA.

After eighteen months of frenetic touring (see 'I'm Movin' On') Elvis was too hot for tiny Sun Studio to handle any more – plus, Sam Phillips was badly short of money. On 21 November 1955,

RCA (Radio Corporation of America) paid $35,000 to Phillips for Elvis's contract, the biggest ever deal in the music industry at that time. The King was in the building.

The Sun sound was inextricably linked with the two musicians who backed Elvis, Scotty Moore and Bill Black. Black died of a brain tumour in 1965; Moore was recently voted one of the fifty greatest guitarists of all time by *Rolling Stone* magazine.

In March 1956, Elvis moved into 1034 Audubon Drive, a ranch-style, three-bedroom home in a posh area of Memphis. His neighbours got so fed up with the fans hanging around that they brought a public-nuisance suit against him. The magistrate threw out the case, saying the fans were not Elvis's responsibility, and in any case, Elvis's house was the only one in the street that was fully paid for. Elvis added a swimming pool to the back yard and fitted fencing decorated with musical staves and notes around the house – a practice run for his next home, Graceland.

'A lot has been written and said about why he was so great, but I think the best way to appreciate his greatness is just to go back and play some of the old records. Time has a way of being unkind to old records, but Elvis's keep getting better and better.' Huey Lewis.

'We flat changed the world of music.' Sam Phillips.

FEVER

Elvis Presley caused two reactions in the 1950s: hysterical adulation, and hysterical condemnation. It was a fever that the whole world was going to catch.

'Elvis had this charisma about him. I don't think anybody could ever put their finger on what he did or how he did it. You could just sit and talk to him for a few minutes and he would mesmerise you.' D.J. Fontana, Elvis's drummer.

'Elvis, who rotates his pelvis ... gave an exhibition that was ... tinged with the kind of animalism that should be confined to dives and bordellos.' US *Daily News*.

The screams of the fans at Elvis's early concerts were so powerful that they would blow dust off the stage curtains. Scotty Moore and Bill Black had to guess where they'd got to in a song by the movement of Elvis's rear end.

'The trouble with going to see Elvis Presley is that you're liable to get killed.' *Detroit Free-Press*.

'[If the media would] stop handling such nauseating stuff, all the Presleys of our land would soon be swallowed up in the oblivion they deserve.' Catholic journal *America*.

Roy Orbison saw Elvis in Odessa, Texas. 'First thing he came out and spat out a piece of gum. His diction was real coarse. I can't overemphasise how shocking he looked and seemed that night.'

Pupils at the Notre Dame Convent in Ottawa had to sign a pledge that they would not attend Elvis's concert. Eight girls were expelled for disobeying.

After a show in Jacksonville, Elvis joked, 'Girls, I'll see you back-stage.' Half the 14,000-strong audience stormed the dressing-room area where police eventually got through to find Elvis clinging for dear life on to the top of one of the showers, his clothes and boots ripped from his body.

'It isn't enough to say that Elvis is kind to his parents ... That still isn't a free ticket to behave like a sex maniac in public.' *Cosmopolitan*.

'When this day is over, an unhealthy chunk of Miami's teenage girls will have unashamedly screamed their lungs out to frank adoration of the biggest freak in modern show-business history. Elvis is a no-talent performer riding the crest of a wave of mass hysteria.' *Miami Herald*.

Elvis played at an air force base near Texarkana. He went outside for some fresh air after the first set and a corporal followed him out and punched him down the steps. Elvis fought back then asked, 'Why did you hit me? I don't even know you.' The corporal replied, 'When you were singing my wife was just going crazy. You can't do that to my wife.'

Just as tens of millions of people were buying their first television sets, Elvis and his sexuality landed right in the middle of their living rooms. Elvis fan and *Northern Exposure* actor John Corbett said, 'The guy looked like he was having sex on stage, humping and sweating and sneering like he's right in the middle of doing it dirty.' Bruce Springsteen put it a bit more politely: 'He was the guy that did it on television for the first time.'

When Elvis played the Dallas Cotton Bowl, D.J. Fontana recalled, 'It looked like a war out there. That's when it really hit me ... I thought, "What's this guy done?"'

'Elvis Presley is morally insane ... We're living in a day of jelly-fish morality.' Reverend Elgena of Des Moines.

At a concert in Los Angeles, Elvis simulated sex with a toy dog called Nipper and the crowd went into a frenzy. Legend has it that it was the theatre manager on that day who, in an attempt to calm people down, first uttered the immortal words, 'Elvis has left the building.'

In Cleveland Elvis provoked mass hysteria when he broke his guitar strings then smashed the instrument on the floor. Police were needed to remove him from the hall.

Elvis developed a technique of undoing his shirt and wriggling out of it super fast, so that grabbing fans could get the shirt without scratching him half to death.

In Kansas City things got so wild that D.J. Fontana was thrown into the orchestra pit.

In Jacksonville, Florida, in 1956, a juvenile-court judge issued a restraining order to stop Elvis making offensive gyrations on stage. Elvis moved only his little finger – and the audience went demented. In a tiny gesture of defiance to the judge in the audience, Elvis altered his trademark farewell to 'Fuck you very much' – inaudible to the fans but registered by his friends in the wings.

Scotty Moore described the sound from those early audiences as 'like when you dive into the water and you hear the rush – it would cancel out all the sound on stage'.

While Elvis was in Germany, DJ Wernher Goetze noisily smashed Elvis records on air and complained that Presley was corrupting German youth 'away from their lederhosen into blue jeans'. German archaeologist Ferdinand Anton described Elvis as 'a throwback to the Stone Age'.

'It was like an earthquake in my neighbourhood. How can a person possess that kind of power that it even comes off the TV and grabs me in this ghetto neighbourhood?' Bobby Womack.

'He shimmied, squirmed and wriggled the mob into a panic which took the efforts of police, sailors and firemen to restrain.' *The Commercial Appeal*.

While Elvis and his girlfriend June Juanico were at a private movie screening in a Memphis cinema, a mob formed outside and tore his car apart. Elvis had to be escorted away by police.

'A hard-working stripper who tried anything like it would find herself a guest of the county.' *Variety*.

Frank Sinatra declared in 1957 that rock and roll was 'a rancid aphrodisiac' sung by 'cretinous goons'. Three years later, his audience figures slipping, he was delighted to have Elvis on his TV show to welcome him home from the army.

The *Miami Herald* charmingly suggested that what the screaming girls in Elvis's audience most needed was a 'solid slap across the mouth'.

'Rock and roll has its place – among the coloured people.' Congressman Emmanuel Celler.

J. Edgar Hoover, director of the FBI, kept a file on Elvis, whom he saw as an icon of rebellion and a threat to just about everything. The file contained basic biographical details, early photos, newspaper clippings and even the names of his girlfriends.

'It was the filthiest and most harmful production ... Indications of the harm Presley did were the two high-school girls whose abdomen and thighs had Presley's personal autograph ... There is also gossip that the Presley Fan Clubs degenerate into sex orgies.' Letter to the FBI from the publisher of the *La Crosse Register*.

Hal Kanter, who directed Elvis in *Loving You*, received phone calls and letters from people outraged that he was putting this 'antichrist' and 'instrument of the devil' on screen.

'The boy is a show-business freak. He'd better save his money while it's pouring in. Chances are in a year or two from now no one will remember him.' *Miami Herald*.

'I've never seen anything like the madness that surrounds Presley.' Natalie Wood.

BLUE SUEDE SHOES

In the 1950s, a time of crew cuts and conformity, Elvis must have been the weirdest – looking kid in Memphis. Black-and-white photographs spare us from some of his gaudier ensembles, but even in monochrome his look is unforgettable.

'Elvis was the most beautiful rock musician of all time.' Bruce Springsteen.

Elvis's obsession with his appearance began in high school. By the time he was sixteen he was attempting to grow sideburns, and grooming his hair with Rose Oil hair tonic and Vaseline.

Elvis's favourite colours were black and pink, at a time when pink was definitely just for girls.

Young Elvis would spend hours with his face pressed to the glass of Lansky's clothing store on Beale Street, the main thoroughfare for the black people of Memphis. The store was full of the sharp styles favoured by the black musicians whom Elvis idolised. Once he had the money, Elvis took to shopping there and remained a loyal customer throughout his life. 'Elvis was our PR man,' Bernard Lansky once explained.

As a teenager Elvis entered a car-safety contest and was pictured in the paper changing a tyre. The contestants around him wore short-sleeved shirts, jeans and work boots. Elvis was dressed in drape jacket, black shirt and loafers.

School peers recollect that the more bizarre-looking and the less like everyone else Elvis became, the more his confidence and self-possession seemed to grow.

A classmate recalled that the one time he saw Elvis wearing blue jeans, Elvis actually apologised, explaining that all his other trousers were in the wash.

When Elvis visited the Tennessee State Employment Security Office in March 1953 to fill out an employment application, the interviewer noted him on the form as 'Rather flashily dressed – "playboy" type'.

A *Louisiana Hayride* radio announcer in 1955 informed his astonished listeners that the Memphis Flash was wearing croco-dile shoes and pink socks.

In March 1956 Elvis bought himself a 14-carat gold ring with the initials EP in white diamonds. It cost $185. He gave it away four months later as a door prize at a charity show.

Elvis liked to wear high or turned-up collars because he thought his neck was too long.

Lansky's once made Elvis a three-quarter-length, fur-trimmed coat in pink leather. After it got ripped Elvis sent it in for repair and clearly forgot about it, as it hangs on the wall of Lansky Bros to this day.

When reporter Fred Danzig interviewed Elvis in 1956, Elvis was wearing blue alligator loafers and a ribbon lavender shirt that Elvis said had cost him $70. Paul Simon saw this shirt in a photograph, and he scoured New York to find one for himself.

By April 1956 Elvis owned 40 suits and 27 pairs of shoes.

'He'd put together clothes that would look awful on you or me, but he could pull it off.' D.J. Fontana, drummer.

Elvis began dying his hair black when he went to Hollywood, to help him look like his idols, Tony Curtis and Rudolph Valentino.

Elvis wore mascara and eye shadow and used to give his girl-friends make-up tips.

Elvis's measurements in 1957 were: waist 32"; inside leg 32½"; hat 7¼"; shirt 15½"; coat 40".

The famous gold suit made its first appearance on 28 March 1957, at the International Amphitheater in Chicago. Colonel Parker had the suit, which cost $2,500, made by Nudie Cohen, who designed stage outfits for country stars such as Hank Snow. Elvis quickly gave up on the trousers; they were very hot and when he dropped onto his knees to the floor the gold would flake off. He preferred to pair the gold jacket with black trousers and gold slip-on shoes with rhinestones on the tassels.

Elvis started having his initials sewn onto his clothes quite early on, and would personalise his wardrobe in this way throughout his life.

When Elvis posed proudly for photographers beside his new gates at Graceland, he wore a yellow jacket, brown trousers, red socks and belt, and white, green and blue shoes decorated with guitar shapes.

Elvis disliked denim and rarely wore it off-screen. It reminded him of poverty.

At a time when etiquette books proclaimed that hair-combing in public was disgusting, Elvis not only combed his hair in public all the time, he also wiped his nose on his sleeve, adjusted his crotch and spat out his chewing gum.

Elvis never wore underpants.

I WANT YOU, I NEED YOU, I LOVE YOU

Elvis's time at Sun Studio produced the most joyous, free, spontaneous music of his life. These ten essential Sun recordings can all be found on the album *Sunrise*.

'My Happiness', 1953
Elvis paid four dollars to record this, as a present for his mother. He's eighteen, he's nervous, but you can hear the voice that shook the world waiting in the wings. This recording was presumed lost for almost thirty years – until an old classmate found it in a drawer.

'That's All Right', 1954
This song is part of music legend (see 'From a jack to a king'). It didn't sound like a 1950s song then, and it doesn't now. It's just a timeless piece of perfection. DJ John Peel, with his usual eye for a classic, says this is his favourite Elvis song.

'Blue Moon Of Kentucky', 1954
Elvis speeded up this bluegrass favourite and added an R & B feel, until Sam Phillips called out, 'Hell, that's different. That's a pop song now, nearly 'bout.'

'Good Rockin' Tonight', 1954
If anybody was in any doubt that 'rock'n'roll' was a euphemism for something else, Elvis masterfully dispels those doubts in this song.

'Just Because', 1954

This is Elvis's mean side coming out. And he does a fine 'We-e-e-e-ll' long before Lulu ever thought of it.

'Milkcow Blues Boogie', 1954

This starts off slow, then Elvis decides he wants to get 'real, real gone' and whizzes through the rest of it, sounding as if he's having the time of his life.

'Baby Let's Play House', 1955

Hiccuping Elvis at his best. He changes the words from 'You may get religion' to 'You may have a pink Cadillac', revealing his ambition and foretelling the purchase of the most famous car in showbiz.

'I'm Left, You're Right, She's Gone', 1955

A melodic country number whose title Elvis never managed to get right in any interview he ever gave.

'Mystery Train', 1955

Sam Phillips said this was 'the greatest thing I ever did on Elvis'. Elvis laughed at the end because he didn't think it was a take, but it was, and the joyful chuckle is the icing on the cake.

'Trying To Get To You', 1955

This is a great R & B song, perfect for the yearning quality in Elvis's voice.

GUITAR MAN

A combination of his passion for music, and simple geography, explains the huge and varied influences on the young Elvis.

Arthur 'Big Boy' Crudup, originator of 'That's All Right', was a hero to Elvis. 'I said if I ever got to the place where I could feel all old Arthur felt, I'd be a music man like nobody ever saw.'

Elvis never had a singing or music lesson in his life.

One of Elvis's first idols was Mississippi Slim, who came from Tupelo and whose brother was a schoolfriend. Elvis used to follow Slim around like a puppy when he performed down at the radio station.

Young Elvis was a frequent visitor to East Trigg Baptist Church, where Reverend Brewster knew how to belt out a gospel number. To the other churchgoers there Elvis was just a shy white kid who'd turn up for the singing.

WDIA was the first radio station in Memphis that was 'programmed exclusively for Negroes'. B.B. King started his life in show business as an announcer there. It played gospel and R & B and it was a constant backdrop in Elvis's life. In 1956, at a WDIA charity event, Elvis told everyone how much he'd benefited from listening to the station.

As a teenager Elvis sometimes went to the Green Owl, a beer joint in Memphis that was primarily a black venue. He particularly liked a musician there who had made a guitar out of a bucket and a broom handle.

One of Elvis's favourite hang-outs was the Home of the Blues record shop on Beale Street. The owner Ruben Cherry was a blues fanatic who stocked pretty much everything. He was the first to stock 'That's All Right' and even lent Elvis money to get to his early concerts. Years later Elvis wrote to Cherry, thanking him for his support, and the letter was read out at Cherry's funeral.

Pop Tunes on Poplar Avenue was another hang-out for Elvis. When he started recording his own songs, he would go in there and see if his records were selling. When Elvis died, the neon sign in front of the store said, 'Elvis, we miss you'.

Ever the drama lover, Elvis owned records by the Italian Mario Lanza, and the Metropolitan Opera.

The country music around Memphis was mostly bluegrass, and Bill Monroe was the star of it. Elvis was nervous about meeting Monroe because he'd dramatically changed Monroe's 'Blue Moon Of Kentucky'. But when Monroe met Elvis at the Grand Old Opry, he complimented the boy and told him he'd just cut his own new version of the song, following Elvis's style.

The teenage Elvis used to love the 'all-night sings', gospel concerts held at Ellis Auditorium in Memphis, but could rarely afford to go. J.D. Sumner, who was then the bass singer for gospel quartet the Blackwood Brothers, used to sneak Elvis in the back to see the show. In the 1970s, Sumner, accompanied by the

Stamps Quartet, was a vital component of Elvis's touring company.

Elvis's favourite gospel quartets were the Blackwood Brothers, the Statesmen and the Jordanaires. The Jordanaires went on to back Elvis in many of his recordings and were known as 'The sound behind the King'.

High Noon Roundup on WMPS Radio used to feature live country and western music. DJ Bob Neal and the performers sat behind big windows so that passers-by could form an audience. Elvis spent many an hour with his nose pressed to the glass.

One of Elvis's favourite singers was Jake Hess, who died in 2004. He was an original member of the Statesmen Quartet and later founded the Imperials. Elvis based his style of ballad singing on Hess's technique. Hess sang 'Known Only To Him' at Elvis's funeral.

Mahalia Jackson was one of Elvis's greatest gospel influences. The King of Rock'n'Roll finally met the Queen of Gospel in 1969, on the set of *Change Of Habit*. He recorded 'An Evening Prayer' in tribute to her on his 1972 LP, *He Touched Me*.

Elvis believed that he really couldn't sing a ballad as well as Pat Boone.

LONG BLACK LIMOUSINE

Elvis's love affair with cars lasted all his life and they became a symbol of his wealth, success and generosity.

In 1951 Elvis took his driving test on his Uncle Travis's 1940 Buick. He passed first time.

The first car that Elvis could consider his own was a 1941 Lincoln bought for him by Vernon Presley in the summer of 1952.

Around Christmas 1955 Elvis bought a tan 1951 Cosmopolitan Lincoln with the proceeds from his performances around the south. He put a rack on top for Bill Black's bass and painted 'Elvis Presley – Sun Records' on the side.

When Bill wrecked the Lincoln under a hay truck in Arkansas, Elvis bought a 1954 pink and white Cadillac, which caught fire soon after on the way to Texarkana. This didn't put him off and his passion for Cadillacs never left him.

The most famous car in showbiz is probably the Cadillac that Elvis bought for his mother and painted pink. She was unable to drive at the time, and she never did learn.

In 1956 Elvis bought a Lincoln Continental Mark II, a car so rare that the dealer ran ads saying that if you saw one on the road, there was a one in two thousand chance that Elvis was behind the wheel.

Elvis owned a Chevrolet one-ton truck that he used to drive around in when he wanted anonymity.

A three-wheeler Messerschmitt was a prize purchase – Elvis called it 'a cool little buggy, if ever there was one'. He later swapped it for a selection of shirts from a clothing store in Memphis.

Elvis was driving his Rolls-Royce in Beverly Hills one day when Jerry Lee Lewis pulled up beside him and looked over at him. Later that day Lewis called Colonel Parker and said, 'Tell Elvis not to drive a Rolls-Royce without a tie.'

In 1962 Elvis bought a Dodge motor home, with double bed and full kitchen, for his trips back and forth between Memphis and Hollywood. He had it customised by George Barris, 'Customiser to the Stars'.

The first 1971 Pontiac Stutz Blackhawk to arrive in Los Angeles had been earmarked for Frank Sinatra, but Elvis persuaded the dealers to let him buy it instead.

Elvis was stopped seven times for speeding.

Elvis's first car when he was in Germany was an old Volkswagen in poor condition. He later gave it to his German karate instructor who kept it as a garden ornament.

Elvis rewarded himself for surviving army manoeuvres with a white BMW 507 sports car. It was one of only 253 ever built and had previously been used by the racing driver Hans Stuck. TV game-show hostess Uschi Siebert presented Elvis with the keys to the car in a press-filled showroom. It was all a PR ploy by BMW and Elvis didn't realise when he signed the contract (written in German) that he had actually only leased the car and had to return it when he left Germany. BMW were not pleased when the car was returned – Elvis had painted it red to alleviate the problem of lipstick messages on the bodywork.

The German press nicknamed Elvis's car 'Der Elviswagen'.

Elvis's most absurd car expenditure was his gold Cadillac. All the accessories were 14-carat gold, and included a record player and a swivel-mounted TV. The car was finished with forty coats of a glitter flake made out of crushed diamonds and fish scales. There were gold lamé curtains at the windows. It had to be guarded by security men every time Elvis took it out and parked it. Elvis finally came to his senses and shut it away in a garage at Graceland. Colonel Parker sent it on tour in 1966 and in Houston alone 40,000 people turned up to look at it.

In 1961 Elvis bought a Thunderbird Landau from Hull-Dobbs Ford in Memphis, after seeing an advert on TV for this special-edition vehicle. He was photographed sitting in the car. Later, when the wheel cover was damaged, Ford happily refunded Elvis the entire $6,000 purchase price: an insignificant sum compared to the value to Ford of the photo.

During one weekend in September 1974 Elvis made five trips to the Schilling dealership on Union Avenue and bought their entire stock of Lincoln Continental Mark IVs, at a cost of over $60,000. He gave all the cars away.

Minnie Person is the lucky star of one of the most famous stories about Elvis's extravagance. She was admiring a Cadillac in a showroom when Elvis walked up to her and asked her if she would like the car. She replied that she would but there was no way she could ever buy it. Don't worry, Elvis replied, 'I just bought it for you.'

One of the last cars Elvis ever bought was a Lincoln Continental he gave to his backing singer Kathy Westmoreland, in the summer of 1977.

A local Memphis car dealer gave Elvis a plaque proclaiming him 'The World's Greatest Car Buyer'. The plaque lists the names of people – all 31 of them – for whom Elvis had bought a car, just from that one dealer.

Despite the quantities in which he bought his cars, Elvis never haggled.

BABY LET'S PLAY HOUSE

It's the second most visited home in the US, after the White House. It's the world's most famous showbiz residence. It is, of course, Graceland, Elvis's much loved home for twenty years.

Graceland was opened to the public on 7 June 1982. In its first year, it attracted over half a million visitors. Visitors now stand at some 650,000 a year.

Graceland was built in 1939 in the Southern colonial style by Dr and Mrs Thomas D. Moore. The house was named after Mrs Moore's great-aunt Grace. The rooms were designed for optimum musical enjoyment, both in terms of space and acoustics, for the benefit of the Moores' daughter Ruth Marie, who would later join the Memphis Symphony Orchestra.

Graceland sits in fourteen acres of hilly woodland south of Memphis, on what was Highway 51 South. Highway 51 South was renamed Elvis Presley Boulevard by the City of Memphis in June 1971. The new road signs were all stolen immediately.

Elvis bought Graceland for $102,500 in March 1957. At the time it was way out in the countryside; now it's swallowed up in the suburb of Whitehaven.

To be authentically Elvis, you have to pronounce the house '*Grey*slun'.

Elvis kept his house keys on a silver shield-shaped key ring with a racecar emblem on the front and his name engraved on the back.

Decorator George Golden was called in straight after the purchase to do up Graceland. Elvis would refurnish and redecorate different parts of the house many times over the years.

During her four-year relationship with Elvis, Linda Thompson redecorated much of Graceland. Even Elvis was said to balk at the extent of her red-fur and leopard-skin look.

Elvis added a lot onto Graceland, including the carport and the racquetball court. When Elvis moved in, the house covered 10,266 square feet. When he died it covered 17,552 square feet.

The famous gates with their guitar motif were made by Veterans Ornamental Iron Works of Phoenix, Arizona, and cost $1,300. The Alabama fieldstone wall surrounding the grounds cost $65,000.

The swimming pool was built in April 1957 by the Paddock Company of California for $8,000. Contrary to myth, it's in the shape of a kidney, not a guitar.

In the grounds of Graceland there was an old house used for storage. Bored one day, Elvis put on his football helmet, got in a bulldozer, knocked it down and set it on fire.

For years Graceland was effectively an open house. Provided you knew someone who knew someone who knew Elvis, you could get in. Elvis was never, for the twenty years that he lived there, on his own.

The living room is subdued (for Elvis), with a 15-foot-long white sofa and white carpet. This is where guests to Graceland would wait for the King to make his entrance.

The door to the music room is decorated with two peacocks in stained glass. Elvis didn't realise that peacocks indoors are considered unlucky. Ironically, his coffin was placed in front of the peacocks at his funeral service.

Elvis liked to put inspirational wall hangings around the house. One reads, 'It is not the critic who counts ... the credit belongs to the man who is actually in the arena.'

The largest room in Graceland was known to Elvis as the den. Staff renamed it the 'Jungle Room' when tours of the house began. Apparently Vernon came home and told Elvis he'd just seen the ugliest furniture ever made in Donald's, a local store. Within thirty minutes Elvis had bought the lot. The room has model animals, a Tiki god, a waterfall and a mirror framed in pheasant feathers. There's even a carpet on the ceiling – which at least was a help when Elvis held recording sessions in there.

The pool room was one of Elvis's favourite retreats. It is covered in hundreds of square yards of colourful pleated fabric – the whole thing looks like a giant psychedelic tent.

Elvis loved gadgets and had a microwave oven way back in 1974.

The old smoke house was generally used for storage, but in the 60s Elvis turned it into a firing range, complete with police target.

The TV room has a bank of three television sets, a bar, a jukebox, a mirrored ceiling and the TCB logo on the wall. Altogether, Elvis had fourteen TV sets at Graceland. It's not known how many he shot . . .

The last record Elvis played in the TV room was Sam Cooke's 'Shake'; it is still on the record player.

Vernon Presley's office was where Elvis held his press conference when he returned home from the army. On the door is a wooden sign which reads: 'Please read and observe. No loafing in office. Strictly for employees only! If you have business here, please take care of it and leave. Vernon Presley.'

Although Elvis owned many guitars in his life, there are just fifteen in the Graceland inventory. On display beside his gold suit is the Gibson J200, one of his favourites, which he used in *Loving You* and in the 1968 TV special.

The trophy room holds the things that meant something to Elvis: gifts from fans, honorary police badges, etc. The sort of stuff that money couldn't buy.

The Meditation Garden was not intended as a burial ground; it was designed at Elvis's request and inspired by his forays into eastern philosophies. The garden now contains the remains of Elvis, Vernon, Gladys and grandmother Minnie Mae, and a plaque in memory of Jesse, Elvis's twin brother. The garden also has the original Presley family monument from the Forest Hill Cemetery.

Elvis's bed is nine feet square with black and gold trimmings. Two pictures hang on either side of it: one of his mother and one of Jesus. The bedroom has two televisions mounted in the ceiling, and there are also security TV monitors as Elvis liked to see what was going on in other parts of the house and down at the gates where the fans were always waiting.

Elvis kept the air conditioning in his bedroom at full blast, and covered the windows with tin foil to aid his nocturnal existence.

The record player in Elvis's bedroom still has the last record he played up there, a gift from J.D. Sumner. It's an acetate of the Stamps singing some of Elvis's favourite gospel songs.

Elvis's bathroom with its padded toilet was his most personal room and nobody could enter without his permission. There were armchairs in there for when he held meetings with his friends, and another chair inside the huge circular shower cubicle. It's also the room where he proposed to his last girlfriend, Ginger Alden.

Up in the attic Elvis kept a closet full of his mother's old clothes. He also kept clothes from his early years and letters from old girl-friends. Hattie, one of the maids, was convinced that there were spirits up there.

Among items on display at the Sincerely Elvis exhibit at Graceland are boxing gloves from Muhammad Ali. Ali has written on them, 'Elvis, you are the greatest.'

The 'Hall of Gold' is so called because the walls are lined from floor to ceiling with the gold and platinum records Elvis received. The awards now spill over into the racquetball court.

The Elvis Presley Automobile Museum opened in 1989, over the road in what is now Graceland Plaza. Among the exhibits are the pink Cadillac that Elvis gave his mother and the Stutz Blackhawk, which was the last car he ever drove.

In the middle of the Automobile Museum is the Highway 51 Drive-In, a mock drive-in movie with real 1957 Chevy seats, which plays scenes from Elvis's films.

The items on display at Graceland make up just a fifth of all Elvis's possessions. The rest of the archive takes up four warehousing facilities. Three are at undisclosed locations around Memphis; the fourth is an earthquakeproof, tornadoproof and fireproof building in the grounds of the house. This is kept at a constant temperature of 66°F to help preserve acetates, papers and clothing.

Most of the archive collection comes from two sources, Vernon Presley and Colonel Parker. Vernon's obsessive hoarding derived from his earlier, poorer days when you held on to receipts to prove you'd paid for things. Parker's collection was bought by Elvis Presley Enterprises in 1990 for an undisclosed sum.

The gates of Graceland open early every day for people who want to visit the Meditation Garden. The 90-minute visitation period is free and ends half an hour before the day's tours begin.

Every Christmas, Graceland is lit up with the original decorations that Elvis used.

Elvis Week, every August, hosts thousands of extra visitors who come to enjoy seminars, memorials and fan events, culminating in the candlelight vigil to commemorate his death.

Tour guides at Graceland are happy to answer questions, but if you try to ask about Elvis's drug use or his sex life, they will reply, 'I don't know. I wasn't there.'

Visitors to Graceland are not allowed upstairs.

Boy George, Bono and Sting have all been spotted doing the Graceland tour.

Over half of visitors are under 35, with a third of them born after Elvis died.

In 1991 Graceland was placed on the National Register of Historic Places.

HEARTBREAK HOTEL

Urban renewal means that many of Elvis's old haunts no longer exist. But there's still plenty besides Graceland to keep an Elvis tourist happy.

Elvis's birthplace in Tupelo is the first item on any self-respecting fan's to-do list. The two-room shack is now the Elvis Presley Museum, and stands on what is now Elvis Presley Drive. Visitors to Tupelo can see Elvis's first school, the church he went to and the shop where Gladys bought his first guitar. And in 2002 the town unveiled a statue of Elvis at thirteen, the age he left.

Back in Memphis, the University of Memphis Bureau of Business and Economic Research estimates that Elvis tourists pump $400 million into the local economy every year.

Graceland-owned Heartbreak Hotel has an average annual occupancy of 80%, some 20% above its local competitors. Its 128 rooms are decorated in blue and gold and show Elvis videos on a loop. There are four themed suites: the Graceland, done up like a mini-mansion; the Hollywood, celebrating Elvis's movie years; the Gold & Platinum, inspired by his recording achievements; and the Burning Love, reflecting his status as a romantic idol. But book early – it fills up a year in advance for Elvis Week.

Sun Studio, on 706 Union Avenue, is known as the Birthplace of Rock'n'Roll. In 2003 the studio became the second building in

Memphis to be designated a National Historic Landmark (Graceland being the first). Sun Studio has tours hourly, every day of the week. After standing where the likes of B.B. King and Jerry Lee Lewis once stood, hearing outtakes from classic recording sessions and, of course, touching Elvis's first microphone, visitors can recover from all the excitement with a milkshake at the Sun Studio soda shop. A little bit of music history for $9.50.

Lansky Bros, Elvis's favourite clothes shop, still exists, though not in the location that Elvis knew. The 'Clothes That Rock' shop on Union Avenue, Memphis features the 'Clothier to the King' line of apparel worn by Elvis in his early years.

There is a statue of Elvis on Beale Street, which manages to look absolutely nothing like him.

True fans seek out the Hotel Chisca at 272 South Main Street. This used to be the home of WHBQ Radio, whose radical DJ Dewey Phillips was the first to play 'That's All Right'. Elvis joined him on air several times.

The Mid-South Fairgrounds, now incorporating a theme park called Libertyland, were among Elvis's favourite haunts and he used to hire out the park after hours. Visitors can take a turn on the Zippin Pippin, the country's second-oldest wooden roller coaster and Elvis's favourite ride. To get the authentic Elvis effect, remember he liked to sit right at the front or right at the back.

Baptist Memorial Hospital, one of the USA's largest hospitals, is a must for the Elvis pilgrim, as this is where Elvis was taken on 16 August 1977 and – after some futile attempts at resuscitation – pronounced dead. He had been hospitalised there several times and, on a happier note, his daughter was born there.

Wealthy fans may want to visit the Elvis Presley Trauma Unit on Jefferson Avenue. Part of Memphis's Regional Medical Center, the unit has received hundreds of thousands of dollars in donations from Elvis fans since its opening in 1983, and any fans donating over $1,000 get their own plaque on the wall.

The Chapel in the Woods, adjacent to Graceland, is the Elvis nut's perfect wedding venue. For $550, you can buy 90 minutes in the chapel and 15 minutes for photos in front of the mansion itself. To respect Elvis's memory, Graceland insists that 'all attire reflect the dignity of the wedding day'. There is also a CD of Elvis love songs available – for $18.95 – only to couples who marry or renew vows at the chapel.

British fans who can't make it across the Atlantic can cheer themselves up at the Fingerprints of Elvis exhibition in Liverpool's Albert Dock. There they can see Elvis's Harley Davidson, stage costumes, karate belts, police badges, army insignia – and some actual fingerprints.

I WANT YOU, I NEE~

He's not called the King for nothin~
rock'n'roll tracks.

'Blue Suede Shoes', 1956
Available on *Elvis Presley*
If someone as prolific as Elvis can have a ~ignature tune, this
quintessential rock'n'roll song must be it – although Elvis
always reckoned Carl Perkins sang it better. Joan Rivers says
it's her favourite Elvis song, because she has a shoe fetish.

'Lawdy Miss Clawdy', 1956
Available on *Elvis Presley*
Elvis thumps this out over an R & B beat and a mean piano,
and sounds simply amazing.

'Shake, Rattle And Roll', 1956
Available on *Elvis Presley*
Producer Steve Scholes requested that for decency's sake Elvis
leave out the verse about the sun shining through a girl's dress,
but in his naivety happily left in 'I'm like a one-eyed cat, peep-
ing in the seafood store.' Ah, the 50s.

'My Baby Left Me', 1956
Available on *Elvis Presley*
This is Elvis on the cusp between the old days and RCA – a Sun
Studio feel with an added drummy chutzpah.

...uts Elvis, and off he goes, his voice rough and
..., banging on that guitar for all he's worth. 'The cats are
...ng wild,' indeed.

'Hound Dog', 1956
Available on *The King Of Rock'n'Roll*
Even though he insisted on doing 30 takes of this song (finally choosing take 28), Elvis still throws himself into it as if he's been shot from a cannon. His final mumble became known in the business as the 'Elvis ending'.

'A Big Hunk O' Love', 1958
Available on *The King Of Rock'n'Roll*
Elvis whoops and hollers his way through this steaming pop song. He was in army uniform when he recorded it, which for some reason makes it even better.

'I Got Stung', 1958
Available on *The King Of Rock'n'Roll*
Still in army gear, Elvis got everyone in the mood for this with a 'Ready on the left, ready on the right, ready on the firing line,' and an upbeat, swinging rock'n'roller was in the can.

'Whole Lotta Shakin' Goin' On', 1970
Available on *Elvis Country*
Elvis was in a bad mood and in a hurry when he recorded this. The result is a manic, aggressive and very, very sexy song.

'Promised Land', 1973
Available on *Promised Land*
A brilliant, fiery race through this Chuck Berry number cocks a snook at all those who thought Elvis's rocking days were over.

FOR THE GOOD TIMES

How does a superstar fill his spare time? Not, apparently, with a cup of tea and a jigsaw.

'He was just a restless soul. He'd get hooked on something and just wear it out. He'd beat it to death, and that's it. He'd never go back to it.' Red West.

One of the first places to benefit from Elvis's new wealth was the Mid-South Fairgrounds. He would hire out the whole place after closing time because his presence in normal hours got too disruptive. Elvis would take friends and fans – up to a hundred people at a time – with him and enjoy the rides until daylight.

Elvis and his Memphis Mafia once played nonstop Yahtzee for four days.

Priscilla once gave Elvis a little racetrack with remote-control cars. Within weeks Elvis had built an entire room onto his house, with a professional slot-car track. He played night after night until he'd had enough and never played again. The room later became the trophy room.

Elvis loved films and often rented out the movie theatre in Memphis. Fans were welcome as well, provided they sat at the back. Among his favourite films were *Patton*, *Shaft* and *On The Waterfront*. He saw *Rebel Without A Cause* 44 times and knew

39

all of James Dean's lines. He also loved the Bond movies, Monty Python and anything with Peter Sellers in it.

Elvis was an avid reader. He once bought 29 books in one go from the Readin' & 'Ritin' shop in Memphis. Titles included *Eyewitness History Of World War II*, *Giants Of Science*, *Jokes For The John* and *Lonely Life*.

Elvis took up karate while in Germany. Instructor Jurgen Seydel came to his house to teach him and found that Elvis had 'an incredible capacity of perception'. From 1971 he was taught by Korean-born Kang Rhee. Rhee named Elvis 'Master Tiger' and eventually awarded him an 8th-degree black belt.

Elvis and Red West established the Tennessee Karate Institute in 1974. Elvis also made copious notes for a karate film he wanted to make, but which never came into being.

Elvis was driving past a petrol station one afternoon when he saw two attendants having a fight. He jumped out of the car and told the fighters, 'If you want trouble, give it to me.' Then he karate-kicked a packet of cigarettes out of one guy's pocket, got back in the car and drove off.

Elvis often rented out the Rainbow Skating Rink in Memphis. He skated like a lunatic – favourite exploits were 'Knock down' when two teams met in the middle of the rink and tried to wipe the floor with each other, and 'Crack the whip', when everyone linked hands and skated round and round as fast as possible. Injuries were commonplace.

Elvis and his friends held fireworks battles in the grounds of Graceland every Christmas and Fourth of July. They set the house on fire at least once.

Motorcycling was one of Elvis's longer-lived passions, and Harleys his favourite bikes. He would persuade the Shelby County police to shut down a stretch of Highway 51 late at night, then race down it at 100mph with his friends. Elvis was an honorary member of the Memphis Motorcycle Club and the American Motorbike Association.

Elvis's most expensive obsession was his passion for horses. He even went out and bought a ranch. In February 1967 Elvis paid almost half a million dollars for the 160-acre Mississippi estate, which he christened the Circle G. He bought trailers for everyone to live in and kitted all of his entourage out with horses and riding gear. For a while it was idyllic, almost like a commune. But then Elvis got bored of ranch life and sold it all for less than he paid for it, just nine months later.

When Elvis got interested in the new trendy sport of racquetball, he quickly built a brand new racquetball court – complete with piano and hot tub – onto Graceland.

Peter Noone of Herman's Hermits once asked Elvis who was his favourite group. Elvis replied, 'The Los Angeles Police Department.' He had detective, police and sheriff badges from all over the United States, and even from abroad, including one from the Royal Papua & New Guinea Constabulary. The badge he really wanted was, ironically, the Federal Narcotics badge, which he would eventually receive from President Nixon.

Elvis built up a good relationship with local Memphis police officers. They sometimes let him go with them on drugs busts, provided he wasn't recognisable. The first time he went out with them, he blended into the background in a bright blue jump suit and a ski mask.

In the space of a few years, Elvis bought at least 250 guns. He lost track of most of them. A husband of one of the secretaries at Graceland sat down on the sofa one day and, finding it a bit lumpy, pulled out a gun from under his cushion. At Sonny West's wedding, Elvis had five guns on him – one under each arm, one in his belt, and one in each boot.

Elvis liked to float flashbulbs in his swimming pool, then take out a gun and shoot them so they'd flash and sink to the bottom.

Elvis always loved playing American football and he formed the EP Enterprises team with friends and associates. Among game plans found at Graceland someone has written, 'EP can't catch too good, but when he does, watch him! He's shifty and fast.'

In 1972 Elvis wrote this note to himself: 'Philosophy for a happy life. Someone to love. Something to look forward to. And something to do.'

BIG BOSS MAN

Elvis thought he owed it all to Colonel Parker. Others aren't so sure.

Andreas 'Dries' Cornelis van Kuijk was born on 26 June 1909 in Breda, Holland. He was the fifth of nine children. His father, Adam, was a liveryman who had met his mother, Maria, while he was in the army.

When Dries was sixteen his father died and he moved to Rotterdam. He worked as a bargeman but was entranced by the ocean-going ships in the port. It wasn't long before he was on board a ship to New Jersey. It is thought that he stowed himself away.

Dries enlisted with the US army – they weren't too fussy about ID papers in those days – and was stationed in Hawaii. When he finally wrote home to his family, the letter was in English and was signed 'Thomas Parker'. This was the name of the captain who had interviewed him at his enlistment.

Years later Elvis's friend Lamar Fike asked Parker, 'How come you never told us you were a Dutchman?' Parker replied, 'You never asked me.'

Parker spent several years with a touring carnival called the Johnny J. Jones Exposition. His special act was dancing chickens, which he achieved by hiding a hotplate under the straw of the chickens' cage.

After marrying Marie Mott in 1935, Parker left the carnival to work for the Tampa Humane Society (presumably he kept quiet about the dancing chickens). He then moved to Nashville and became manager to country singer Eddy Arnold.

Jimmy Davis was an old hillbilly singer and a friend of Parker's from carnival days. When Davis became Louisiana governor, he gave Parker an honorary commission. Parker was known as the Colonel from that day onwards. Funnily enough, in March 1961, Governor Buford Ellington of Tennessee made Elvis an honorary colonel. Elvis didn't deem it necessary to use his title.

In 1953 Eddy Arnold fired Parker for unknown reasons. Parker then hooked up with Hank Snow and they created Jamboree Attractions, which soon became one of the biggest booking agencies in the South. But the partnership split up acrimoniously when Parker, without Snow, signed a new young talent. His name was Elvis Presley.

Parker first met Elvis in February 1955, in a Memphis coffee shop. His first words to him were, 'You got a manager, son?' By spring Parker had booked Elvis onto a Jamboree Attractions tour, and was ready to pounce.

Elvis was legally a minor in 1955, which meant any contract had to be signed by his parents. Vernon was a pushover but Gladys was suspicious of the Colonel. Parker enlisted the help of 'the Duke of Paducah', squeaky-clean country comedian Whitey Ford, to meet Gladys backstage at one of Elvis's shows and tell her what a fine Christian gentleman the Colonel was.

Elvis and Parker signed their contract on 15 August 1955. Parker was described as 'special adviser . . . to negotiate and assist in any way possible the buildup of Elvis Presley as an artist [and] . . . to negotiate all renewals on existing contracts.'

Parker set about creating the deal to make RCA Elvis's record company, and Hill & Range his music publishers. Steve Scholes, RCA's director of country music, put his neck on the line to offer $25,000. Hill & Range offered a further $15,000. With a $40,000 offer in place, Parker paid Sam Phillips an agreed $35,000 and gave $5,000 to Elvis.

Elvis signed with RCA on 21 November 1955. The next day he sent a telegram to Parker in which he promised to stick with him through thick and thin, and said he loved him like a father.

On 8 January 1956, Elvis's 21st birthday, Parker gave Elvis a new contract to sign as an adult. It ratified all previous contracts and gave the Colonel 25% of Elvis's earnings.

Once Parker became Elvis's manager, he didn't take on anyone else. As his assistant Trude Forsher put it, 'The Colonel lived and breathed Elvis twenty-four hours a day.'

Parker didn't believe in spending money on decent support acts, so he filled shows with third-rate has-beens who had to endure the crowd howling for Elvis throughout their acts. He once rounded up some dwarfs from a carnival in Chicago and brought them on as the Elvis Presley Midget Fan Club.

Parker showed his nerve when he demanded $100,000 for Elvis to star in *Love Me Tender*. When the producer said that even Jack Lemmon didn't get that kind of money, Parker replied that maybe Lemmon should get a new manager.

Once Elvis got to Hollywood and was mixing with other stars, Parker grew afraid that Elvis would realise how unusual his contract with Parker was and try to dump him. Parker recruited his brother-in-law Bitsy Mott and young actor Nick Adams to hang around Elvis and keep 'subversives' at bay. He isolated Elvis so effectively that when songwriter Mike Stoller knocked on the door of Elvis's hotel suite one day, Elvis greeted him nervously and said the Colonel wouldn't approve of a one-to-one meeting.

Parker was certain that he could keep the Elvis frenzy going while his client was in the army. He said during Elvis's draft procedure, 'I consider it my patriotic duty to keep Elvis in the 90% tax bracket.'

Parker's view was, 'If you want to see Elvis Presley, buy a ticket.' Elvis was not allowed to give any performances for his fellow soldiers while in the army. Parker even turned down an invitation for Elvis to sing at the White House – not even the President was getting Elvis for nothing. Similarly, Elvis never gave encores – always leaving them wanting more.

Once during the filming of *Blue Hawaii*, Parker ran shouting and yelling into the middle of a scene, pointed at Elvis's wristwatch, and demanded, 'If you want the watch in, you'll have to pay us another ten grand.' No wonder Elvis's performance was a little stilted.

In public, producer Hal Wallis admired Parker as a 'supersalesman', but in private he said, 'I'd rather try and close a deal with the devil.'

Parker had no interest in developing Elvis's acting talent. His Hollywood formula for the 1960s was simple – three films a year, with plenty of singing. He once boasted that he didn't read scripts: 'All we want is songs for an album.'

In 1966, demand for Elvis films and records fell sharply. Parker promptly negotiated a new contract that gave him 50% of Elvis's earnings.

As a side earner, Parker would insist on getting a credit in Elvis's movies – as adviser, consultant or technical director – and the accompanying salary, for doing absolutely nothing.

When a TV executive came to Parker offering $50,000 for a single prime-time appearance by Elvis, Parker responded, 'That'll be just fine for me, but how much are you going to give the boy?'

The extent of Parker's role in Elvis's wedding is disputed (some say he told Elvis to get married for publicity purposes), but it was a rushed affair with a savagely brief guest list, which caused huge ructions among Elvis's entourage. He also refused to let the happy couple have the honeymoon in Europe that they wanted, saying it would upset fans if Elvis went there without performing. Why Elvis didn't insist on the wedding he and Priscilla wanted is an enduring mystery.

Parker was a competent hypnotist. He liked to get staff members to act like chickens, and once had the Memphis Mafia all barking like dogs. However, theories that Parker kept Elvis hypnotised for twenty years should be taken with a pinch of salt.

Elvis stood up to the Colonel on just a handful of occasions. One was the 1968 TV special, which Parker had wanted dull and Christmassy and which ended up one of Elvis's finest, rawest performances. Then a few months later, Parker didn't want Elvis to record a particular song because of a rights disagreement. The song in question was 'Suspicious Minds'.

In 1969 Elvis returned to live performing at the International Hotel in Las Vegas. Alex Shoofey, the International's general manager, came to Parker in the hotel dining room and offered a five-year contract, in which Elvis would play the International in February and August each year and earn $125,000 a week. Parker scribbled some terms on the red tablecloth, but he ignored inflation and he tied Elvis in long term. Alex Shoofey signed his agreement on the tablecloth and promptly told the press it was 'the best deal ever made in this town'. Not, perhaps, for Elvis.

Parker's lifelong gambling habit became an addiction in the Vegas years. He moved into the International Hotel, where he had a fancy suite with all the privileges of a high roller, and proceeded to lose over a million dollars a year on the roulette tables.

In the 70s, most of Elvis's income came from touring. In February 1972 he signed away one-third of his tour profits to Parker, 'in consideration of ... [Parker's] complete organising of tours'. It was, in fact, the promoter Jerry Weintraub who did the organising.

In 1973, after a big row, Elvis fired Parker, but Parker said he was owed several millions and wouldn't go without it. Elvis went into a weeklong drug-fuelled strop that culminated in a teenage girl almost overdosing. And who did Elvis call to sort out the mess and keep the papers away? Colonel Parker.

The Colonel turned down endless offers for Elvis to tour abroad because Parker was an illegal immigrant without a passport.

In 1973, RCA bought the masters – and royalty rights – of all Elvis's previous recordings for $5.4 million. Jack Soden of EPE (Elvis Presley Enterprises) describes this as a deal 'right up there with the Indians selling Manhattan for twenty-four dollars'. Seven years later a lawyer for the Presley estate, Blanchard Tual, concluded that Colonel Parker and RCA were 'probably guilty of collusion, conspiracy, fraud [and] misrepresentation'.

In 1974 Parker set up Boxcar Enterprises to handle the merchandising business. Parker was on 40% of merchandising income; Elvis was on 15%.

When Joe Esposito phoned Parker to tell him that Elvis had died, Parker's first words were 'Oh, dear God'. Then, after a pause: 'Nothing has changed. This won't change anything.'

Within a day of the death Parker had got Vernon Presley, the executor of Elvis's will, to agree to keep all the deals made with Elvis as they were. He also signed a deal with the merchandising company Factors Inc that meant Parker would take 78% of the proceeds of the forthcoming souvenir boom.

At Elvis's funeral, Parker wore a Hawaiian shirt and a baseball cap. At the cemetery he wandered away from the graveside and sat by himself on a police motorcycle.

After Vernon's death in 1979, the courts got involved and, after a lot of wrangling, a deal was struck whereby Parker severed all connections with the Presley estate for a hefty sum.

Tom Parker died in January 1997. Opinion on Parker remains divided: some believe he was a brilliant promoter and tireless manager; others think that the career of a naive genius was nearly destroyed by his greed.

Soldier boy

When Elvis was drafted into the army he was genuinely afraid that by the time he returned to civilian life everybody would have forgotten him . . .

Elvis received his draft notice in December 1957. He was told to report for induction on 20 January 1958, but managed to get a two-month deferment to complete filming on *King Creole*.

Elvis was inducted into the army on 24 March 1958. His serial number was 53310761. His medical was carried out at Kennedy Veterans Hospital in Memphis, where he was pronounced 'A1 – suitable for all military duties'.

Private Presley's last words as he got on the bus from Memphis to Fort Chaffee, Arkansas, were 'Goodbye, you long black son-ofabitch.' They were addressed to his Cadillac.

At Fort Chaffee, Elvis was given several inoculation injections, an aptitude test and the world's most famous haircut, for which he paid 65 cents.

After four days at Fort Chaffee, Elvis went to Fort Hood, Texas, for basic training. There he gained medals for expertise with a carbine rifle and with tank weapons.

During his time at Fort Hood Elvis lived off base in Killeen, where his parents came to stay. This was in accordance with army regulations as Elvis's parents were classed as dependants.

On army leave in June 1958, Elvis went to Studio B in Nashville for a recording session – his last of the decade. He turned up in uniform.

The biggest trauma of Elvis's army career was the death of his mother, Gladys, on 14 August 1958. She died of heart problems and hepatitis, exacerbated by alcohol and pills. At the funeral Elvis was inconsolable and cried out, 'Everything I have is gone.'

On 22 September 1958 Elvis left America for Germany, to do an 18-month stint with the US Third Army Division. He boarded the USS *Randall* at the Military Ocean Terminal in Brooklyn, having walked up and down the gangplank eight times for the benefit of the assembled photographers. The ship docked at Bremerhaven, West Germany, on 1 October.

From Bremerhaven Elvis took the troop train to Friedberg and the Ray Barracks, which had once housed Hitler's SS troops. Elvis had bed number 13 in barracks 3707.

On 2 October Elvis held a press conference in the mess hall. The hall had been spruced up for the occasion and Elvis had to change his uniform jacket after leaning on a newly painted window frame.

Elvis's first assignment was to Company D of the 1st Medium Tank Battalion, 32nd Armor, whose motto was 'Victory or Death'.

Elvis soon brought father Vernon, grandmother Minnie Mae, and friends Red West and Lamar Fike out to Germany. He gained permission to live off base and they all moved to the beautiful old town of Bad Nauheim, first to the Hilberts Park Hotel, then to the posher Hotel Grünewald, where he had to rent an extra room just for the fan mail.

In November Elvis went on special training manoeuvres in snowy Grafenwöhr, near the border of Czechoslovakia. His proximity to Communist territory caused a stir: East German paper *Neues Deutschland* described Elvis as 'a Cold War weapon', while the Soviet press accused him of being part of the West's 'ideological battle' to subvert Communist youth. In Leipzig, a gang of youths called the Elvis Presley Hound Dogs were arrested for committing anti-State acts by performing Elvis songs.

On 27 November Elvis was promoted to Private First Class, receiving his first stripe and a salary increase, from $78 to $99.37 a month.

The Hotel Grünewald was used to elderly, sedate residents and Elvis's boisterous behaviour, piano playing and water fights in the hallways didn't go down too well. So in January 1959 Elvis rented out a house at 14 Goethestrasse. The canny owner, Frau Pieper, charged him over 1000 Deutschmarks a month, about five times the going rate.

Elvis hired a piano from the Kuehlwetter music shop and played most evenings. He had to keep the living-room shutters closed to stop passers-by calling out requests.

Elvis's hairdresser in Bad Nauheim was Herr Leutzer of the Salon Jean Hemer. His dentist was Dr Atta. Both these men would open in the evening especially for Elvis. He also had his own taxi driver, Joseph Wehrheim, who had once been the chauffeur for the newspaper magnate William Hearst.

At 14 Goethestrasse Elvis put a sign on the door, in German, which said: 'Autographs between 7.30 – 8.30 p.m.'

On 1 June 1959 Elvis was promoted to Specialist Fourth Class, and his pay rose to $122.30 a month. Celebrations were muted as he spent a week in hospital with tonsillitis.

Vernon caused scandal in Bad Nauheim by conducting an affair with Dee Stanley, the wife of an NCO stationed in Friedberg. He would later marry Dee and move her and her three children to Memphis.

On leave, Elvis liked to go to Munich or Paris. In Paris he particularly liked the Lido where the Bluebell Girls performed, because they were mainly English speakers.

On 20 January 1960 Elvis was promoted to Sergeant and placed in command of a three-man reconnaissance team. His pay was now $145 a month. His platoon leader stated, 'I said before that Sergeant Presley was a good soldier, and now I can add that he's a fine NCO.'

Elvis's last army assignment was a 'Winter Shield' exercise in Wildflicken.

On 1 March Elvis held a press conference in the Services Club of the Third US Armored Division at Friedberg. Captain J. Mawn read a citation from Elvis's commanding officer, which described Elvis's 'initiative, drive, and cheerful performance of duty, [bringing] great credit on himself, his unit, and the United States Army'.

Elvis left Germany on 2 March 1960 on a Military Air Transport plane. The flight home gave him his one and only contact with British soil, on a fuelling stopover at Prestwick Airport in Scotland. A plaque at the airport marks the event.

Elvis arrived back at McGuire Airforce Base near Fort Dix, New Jersey in a blizzard. He was handed a mustering-out cheque of $109.54, which he gave to Colonel Parker.

When John Lennon was told that Elvis had died, he replied, 'Elvis died the day he went into the army.'

JUST PRETEND

Elvis was no Laurence Olivier, as he was the first to admit, but he had an incredible screen presence and great timing, and his acting visibly matured through his 1950s films. Then he came out of the army and Hollywood stuck him in fluffy, formulaic films and did the unthinkable – they took the sex out of Elvis Presley.

'[Elvis] was not an actor. We did not sign him as a second Dean or second Brando. We signed him as the number one Elvis Presley.' Producer Hal Wallis.

Elvis starred in 31 feature films between 1956 and 1969. He became the highest-paid movie star on earth. In all, his films made some $400 million at the box office.

In March 1956, Elvis arrived at Hal Wallis's studio for a screen test. First he had to sing 'Blue Suede Shoes' with a prop guitar, just to see if he looked good on screen. He did. 'One felt it as an awesome thing – like an earthquake in progress. To deny his talent would have been foolish, like sticking your finger into a live socket and denying the presence of electricity.' Alan Weiss, screenwriter.

Then Elvis acted a scene from *The Rainmaker*, starring Katherine Hepburn and Burt Lancaster. Elvis thought that this serious drama was going to be his first film – he even said so to interviewers – but Colonel Parker thought the part was too small.

In April, Elvis signed a non-exclusive contract with Hal Wallis and Paramount to make seven movies in seven years (his first film would actually be with 20th Century Fox). Elvis said, 'It's a dream come true.'

Elvis and his entourage moved into the Beverly Wilshire Hotel when they first came to Hollywood. Elvis called it 'the old folks' home' and, some major water fights and room wrecks later, they moved.

At his first meeting with director Hal Kanter, Elvis said he hoped he wouldn't have to smile too much in the movies because he'd been studying the likes of Brando and Dean and they never smiled – 'That's why people remember them.'

Elvis chose to impress Hal Kanter by reciting from memory the whole of General MacArthur's farewell speech to Congress.

Elvis's first film was originally called *The Reno Brothers*. They slipped in the song 'Love Me Tender', changed the name of the movie, and the die was cast.

When Elvis turned up for the first day of filming on 23 August, he had learned the entire script, his part and everyone else's, off by heart.

Scotty Moore and Bill Black, Elvis's backing musicians, had to audition for the part of Elvis's backing musicians in *Love Me Tender*. They didn't get it. They would, however, appear in *Loving You*, *Jailhouse Rock* and *King Creole*.

Love Me Tender opened on 15 November 1956 at the Paramount Theater in New York. A 40-foot cardboard cutout of

Elvis adorned the building. It being a Thursday, truant officers were in attendance.

Love Me Tender recovered its production costs in three days. It had the second-highest first-week earnings of 1956, after James Dean's *Giant*.

Love Me Tender may have been a hit with the fans, but the critics were less impressed. *Harvard Lampoon* awarded Elvis 'Worst Supporting Actor' for his performance. And *Time* magazine sniffed, 'Is it a sausage? . . . Is it a Walt Disney goldfish? . . . Is it a corpse? . . . A peculiar sound emerges. A rusty foghorn?'

Hollywood thought the two teeth on either side of Elvis's front teeth were too small, so he wore cosmetic caps in front of the camera. But he couldn't eat with them in and, as Elvis was always eating, he left the caps all over the place and got through dozens of pairs.

Vernon and Gladys Presley appeared as extras in *Loving You*, and are clearly seen in the audience as Elvis sings 'Got A Lot O' Livin' To Do'. Because of this, Elvis refused ever to watch the film again after Gladys's death.

When Elvis made *Jailhouse Rock* for MGM, he was paid $250,000 plus profits. Profit share was a demand that only the biggest stars could make.

Elvis's contract with MGM included the clause, 'Can never cut his hair off without our permission'. He had to wear a 'butch cut' wig for his prison role in *Jailhouse Rock*. This entailed making a cast of Elvis's head. When the make-up artist cut the cast to remove it, he accidentally cut some of the famous Presley locks.

When Elvis saw the hair falling onto his shoulder he said, 'Man, there's Frankie Avalon fans *every* place.'

The dance sequence to *Jailhouse Rock*'s title song is one of the most famous in film history. Choreographer Alex Romero wanted a Fred Astaire-style routine, but Elvis said it just wasn't him. Romero got Elvis to dance for him there and then and came back the next day with a new routine, perfect for Elvis.

Elvis's co-star in *Jailhouse Rock*, Judy Tyler, was killed in a car crash before the movie was released.

Film technicians expected the worst from Elvis, but many are on record as saying they found him always punctual, prepared and professional. Co-star Millie Perkins said that Elvis never used his star power to get his way on a film set.

King Creole is generally thought to be Elvis's best movie. After filming, Elvis said to director Michael Curtiz, 'Thank you very much, Mr Curtiz, now I know what a director is.'

Elvis's membership number for the Screen Actors' Guild was 42838.

Throughout the 1960s Elvis lived in several homes around Hollywood, including a house on Perugia Way in Bel Air owned by the Shah of Iran, and a house in Palm Springs where he had Bob Hope and Bing Crosby as neighbours.

Flaming Star was banned in South Africa because Elvis played a mixed-race character.

In 1992 the University of Mississippi taught a course called '*Blue*

Hawaii: The Polynesian Novels and Hawaiian Movies of Melville and Elvis'. I'm not making this up.

The *Blue Hawaii* soundtrack album sold two million copies. The people had spoken – they wanted sunshine, they wanted songs, and who cared what Elvis wanted.

In *Kissin' Cousins* Elvis played two roles, for one of which he had to wear a blond wig. Some days on set, he was so ashamed that he didn't want to come out of his dressing room. By this stage he was often physically sick when he read his scripts.

Viva Las Vegas was called *Love In Las Vegas* in Europe. It was banned by the Catholic authorities on the Mediterranean island of Gozo.

Hal Wallis once admitted to using the profits from Elvis films to fund 'serious' projects. For Elvis movies, he told screenwriter Alan Weiss simply to write a framework for twelve songs.

In *Roustabout*, Elvis wanted the Jordanaires to sing one of the songs with him. But, said director John Rich, Elvis was singing the song while riding his motorbike; where would you put the backing singers? Elvis replied, 'Same damn place you put the band.' Maybe they should have got Elvis to write the scripts.

Tickle Me, despite being declared 'the silliest, feeblest and dullest vehicle for the Memphis Wonder in a long time' by the *New York Times*, still saved its producers Allied Artists from bankruptcy, and was the studio's third-highest grossing film ever.

Director Gene Nelson was given fifteen days to shoot *Harum Scarum*. Elvis offered to pretend to be ill to give Nelson some more time. Even Colonel Parker was stunned by the film and told

MGM that it would take 'a 55th cousin of P.T. Barnum' to have any hope of selling it.

While filming *Harum Scarum*, Elvis enjoyed his Valentino look so much that he would keep his make-up and turban on right up until bedtime.

Elvis got increasingly plastic-looking and desexualised in the mid-60s (he recovered spectacularly by 1968). By the time he made *Spinout*, *Time* magazine commented that his hair was 'like a swatch of hot buttered yak wool'.

When George Klein asked Elvis what his latest movie (*Easy Come, Easy Go*) was about, Elvis replied, 'Same film, different location.'

'[Colonel Parker] had a golden goose and he kept wanting to turn out the same eggs.' Mike Stoller.

In *Clambake* Elvis wore a white suit that was cut into pieces after filming. The pieces were then packaged in the snappily titled box set *Elvis: The Other Sides – Worldwide Gold Award Hits, Volume 2*.

Elvis's portrayal of an American Indian in *Stay Away Joe* earned him a nomination for a Golden Turkey Award, in the category of 'Most Ludicrous Racial Impersonation in Hollywood History'. He was kept off the winning spot by Marlon Brando and his Okinawan impression in *The Teahouse Of The August Moon*.

Elvis's favourite co-star was Shelley Fabares, who played opposite him in *Girl Happy*, *Spinout* and *Clambake*. His least favourite was Mary Tyler Moore from *Change Of Habit*.

Elvis's character in *Change Of Habit* was Dr John Carpenter – a name Elvis subsequently used at times to help him travel incognito.

Even Elvis fans eventually began to grow tired of his films. By the late 60s, distributors in Europe and in some parts of America were refusing to take Elvis pictures. The country that remained loyal to Elvis movies for the longest was India.

In 1974 Barbra Streisand approached Elvis to star alongside her in a remake of *A Star Is Born*. Elvis was really excited about it but Colonel Parker rejected it – no way was Elvis going to have second billing to Streisand.

'He was perfect for Hollywood and a casualty of Hollywood. He was perfect for Hollywood in that they could put him in anything and he would draw, and he was victimised by Hollywood for the same reason.' Mike Stoller.

'I'd like to make one good film before I leave. I know this town's laughing at me.' Elvis, 1968.

I want you, I need you, I love you

When Hollywood got it right, they really got it right. Here are the ten essential Elvis movie songs.

'Love Me Tender', 1956
> Available on *The King Of Rock'n'Roll: The Complete 50s Masters*
> This ballad is forever linked with Elvis, and was, unfortunately, the best thing about the film. He later used it in his concerts as an excuse to kiss half the audience.

'Mean Woman Blues', 1957
> Available on *The King Of Rock'n'Roll*
> This bluesy rocker with a hint of menace is perfectly suited to Elvis, and the highlight of *Loving You*.

'(Let Me Be Your) Teddy Bear', 1957
> Available on *The King Of Rock'n'Roll*
> Another classic from *Loving You*. Is there anybody on the planet who doesn't know the words to this song? And where would karaoke nights be without it?

'Jailhouse Rock', 1957
> Available on *The King Of Rock'n'Roll*
> What a great, funny, exciting bit of rock'n'roll. D.J. Fontana apparently imagined he was a prisoner breaking up rocks when he did the opening drums. The dance sequence in the film was Elvis's finest Hollywood moment.

'(You're So Square) Baby I Don't Care', 1957
Available on *The King Of Rock'n'Roll*
Bill Black just couldn't get the opening right on this; he hurled his new electric bass to the floor and walked out. Elvis just laughed, picked it up and played it himself. His performance of this song in *Jailhouse Rock* is the epitome of beautiful young Elvis.

'King Creole', 1958
Available on *The King Of Rock'n'Roll*
From the instantly recognisable opening bars to Elvis's deep, growling delivery, this is a great song from Elvis's best film.

'Can't Help Falling In Love', 1961
Available on *30 #1 Hits*
A classic ballad that began as a tune in a music box in *Blue Hawaii*. Elvis went on to end most of his 1970s shows with this song.

'Return To Sender', 1962
Available on *30 #1 Hits*
From *Girls! Girls! Girls!*, this is as familiar as the back of your hand. Sometimes a cigar is just a cigar, and sometimes a perfect pop song is just a perfect pop song. Opera star Bryn Terfel chose this song as one of his *Desert Island Discs*.

'Bossa Nova Baby', 1963
Available on *Second To None*
This song from *Fun In Acapulco* is great – camp, latin, full of chicks and cats digging the band. Austin Powers would have loved this. If you can keep your feet still during this song, then you're already dead.

'Clean Up Your Own Back Yard', 1968

Available on *The Trouble With Girls* soundtrack

This was the light at the end of the long, bleak tunnel of the mid-60s movies. It's funky, it's eloquent, and Elvis actually enjoys a movie song for the first time in a long time.

RELEASE ME

There are some great Elvis movie moments; his charisma could floor an elephant. But, with a few exceptions, the storylines were truly *atrocious*. 'Release me' pretty much sums up how Elvis – and the audience – felt by the end of his Hollywood years.

Love Me Tender, 1956
Clint Reno is a singing hillbilly who marries his brother's fiancée and gets shot, not a moment too soon.

Loving You, 1957
Deke Rivers is a singer with a thing about teddy bears who makes it to the top thanks to an outfit that Village People would die for.

Jailhouse Rock, 1957
Vince Everett is a singing tractor driver who survives a spell in jail to find stardom and make cable-knit jumpers sexy again.

King Creole, 1958
Danny Fisher is a nightclub singer who puts the New Orleans mobsters in their place and wins stardom and self-respect through punching a lot of people.

GI Blues, 1960
Tulsa Maclean is a singing soldier who takes on a bet to win over an ice maiden and also croons to hand puppets in German.

Flaming Star, 1960

Pacer Burton is a singing half-white, half-Kiowa man torn between his loyalties, who decides to die before the other Kiowa notice he doesn't look remotely like them.

Wild In The Country, 1961

Glenn Tyler is a singing delinquent who narrowly escapes jail and the wrong woman to become a literary genius, hopefully a screenwriter.

Blue Hawaii, 1961

Chad Gates is a singing ex-GI who turns his back on his dad's pineapple business to play with girls in the surf and wear loud shirts.

Follow That Dream, 1962

Toby Kwimper is a singing halfwit whose family of waifs and strays sets up home on a stretch of beach for no particular reason.

Kid Galahad, 1962

Walter Gulick is a singing mechanic who discovers his hidden talent as a singing boxer.

Girls! Girls! Girls!, 1962

Ross Carpenter is a singing tuna fisherman who wins the girl with his surprising ability to speak fluent Chinese.

It Happened At The World's Fair, 1963

Mike Edwards is a singing crop-duster pilot who falls for a nurse and gets kicked by small children.

Fun In Acapulco, 1963

Mike Windgren is a singing trapeze artist who solves his women problems by jumping off a cliff.

Kissin' Cousins, 1964

Jody Tatum and Josh Morgan are singing identical cousins who wrestle a lot, sometimes with each other, sometimes with movie-set stand-ins by mistake.

Viva Las Vegas, 1964

Lucky Jackson is a singing racing-car driver who wins both the race and a swimming teacher who keeps forgetting to put her skirt on.

Roustabout, 1964

Charlie Rogers is a singing, leather-clad biker who saves a carnival and gets a girl, all in the time it takes for his bike to be fixed.

Girl Happy, 1965

Rusty Wells is a singer (!) hired by a gangster to keep his daughter away from men. On reflection this may not have been a sensible decision on the part of the gangster.

Tickle Me, 1965

Lonnie Beale is a singing rodeo rider who marries a fitness trainer after unmasking the baddies who were after her granddaddy's gold. Same old, same old.

Harum Scarum, 1965

Johnny Tyrone is a singing movie star who is kidnapped in a country with lots of pretty slave girls and is ordered to kill the king. He doesn't, obviously.

Frankie And Johnny, 1966
Johnny is a singing riverboat gambler who gets into trouble when he mixes a redhead with a blonde.

Paradise, Hawaiian Style, 1966
Rick Richards is a singing helicopter pilot who executes daring rescues and enthrals the local girls with his chopper.

Spinout, 1966
Mike McCoy is a singing racing-car driver (again) who fights off the nuptial intentions of three women and also, incredibly, wins the car race.

Easy Come, Easy Go, 1967
Ted Jackson is a singing frogman who is out to retrieve some sunken treasure before the villains find it. Luckily he has a go-go dancer to help him.

Double Trouble, 1967
Guy Lambert is a singing bandleader who masterfully deals with obsessed fans, diamond thieves and assassins and still finds time to sing 'Old Macdonald'.

Clambake, 1967
Scott Heywood is a singing oil heir who pretends to be a water-ski instructor to find true love. Flipper the dolphin gets most of the best lines.

Stay Away Joe, 1968
Joe Lightcloud is a singing Navajo Indian who rescues his reservation while avoiding a shotgun marriage and wrestling with a bull.

Speedway, 1968

Steve Grayson is a singing stock-car driver who manages to divert the beautiful tax inspector's attention away from the size of his wallet.

Live A Little, Love A Little, 1968

Greg Nolan is a singing photographer who is taught the importance of love by a girl with a big dog.

Charro!, 1969

Jess Wade is a reformed gunslinger with a beard and no interest in singing, except over the opening credits.

The Trouble With Girls, 1969

Walter Hale is a singing manager of a troupe of entertainers. He solves a murder and gets a girl who clearly agrees that he looks completely fantastic in his white suit.

Change Of Habit, 1969

John Carpenter is a doctor who falls in love with an undercover nun. Did I mention he sings?

'I've had people ask me was I gonna sing in the movies ... I'm not, I mean as far as I know, 'cause I took strictly an acting test and I wouldn't care too much about singing in the movies.' Elvis, April 1956.

I'M WITH A CROWD BUT SO ALONE

Sinatra had his Rat Pack; Elvis had his Memphis Mafia. Supporters and sycophants, protectors and parasites, friends and flunkeys – they were all of these things between them. The hard thing is working out who was which.

When former girlfriend Barbara Hearn was working on a teen magazine, she asked Elvis to name his likes and dislikes. Among likes was 'having lots of people around me at all times'. Among dislikes was 'being alone'.

Red West was a fiery-tempered footballer at Humes High School. Red once rescued Elvis from a gang of lads who weren't impressed with his constant hair combing. He became Elvis's friend and, later, bodyguard, and appeared on screen with Elvis a few times, usually in fight scenes.

Sonny West – Red's cousin – was three years younger than Elvis. They first met just before Elvis went into the army, and Sonny was 'initiated' into the group at one of Elvis's wild ice-skating sessions.

Elvis met George Klein in the eighth grade. Elvis would point to Klein in the school photo that hung on the wall at Graceland and say, 'He was one of the few guys that was nice to me in school.' Klein was one of Memphis's top DJs for years, and used his connections to find lots of pretty women to bring up to Graceland.

When Elvis was posthumously inducted into the Rock'n'Roll Hall of Fame, it was Klein who gave the acceptance speech on his behalf.

Jerry Schilling first met Elvis in 1954, when he was invited to join in a game of touch football. He was the most intellectual of the group surrounding Elvis. He later went out with Myrna Smith of the Sweet Inspirations.

Lamar Fike was a fan who managed to get an introduction to Elvis and won his friendship with his good humour. He was so devoted to Elvis that he tried to enlist on the day that Elvis was drafted, but was rejected due to his 300-pound frame. He went to Germany anyway.

Richard Davis joined the group in 1961. He started as a general gofer and became wardrobe manager and Elvis's movie stand-in.

Charlie Hodge met Elvis briefly backstage in 1957 when Charlie was playing in a country quartet, but they became close friends in the army. In 1960 Elvis was getting on a train bound for Hollywood when he asked out of the blue if Charlie would like to go with him. Charlie got on the train in the clothes he stood up in and stayed with Elvis for seventeen years. He sang harmony with Elvis and handed him his drinks and scarves during all the 70s shows.

Joe Esposito was from Chicago and met Elvis in the army. He impressed Vernon in Germany by collecting hotel bills and other receipts so that, for the first time ever, Elvis actually wrote something off against tax. He became Elvis's 'foreman' and pretty much ran things for a long time.

Alan Fortas was a footballer and a friend of George Klein. Elvis took to him straight away and nicknamed him 'Hog Ears'.

Marty Lacker was another friend of Klein's and first joined the group in Hollywood. He was personal secretary to Elvis and best man, with Joe Esposito, at his wedding.

Elvis's cousins, Gene, Billy and Junior Smith, were on the payroll. Junior never recovered from his experience in Korea and met an alcohol-related death aged 28 in 1961. Gene looked after Elvis's cars, and Elvis just felt sorry for Billy, who was rather small.

The group had one female member. Hairdresser Patti Parry saw Elvis in his Rolls-Royce on Santa Monica Boulevard one day and won him over by pretending not to recognise him. She became one of the guys and would claim to be the only Jewish girl to know every gospel song.

Everybody theoretically had 'jobs'. The salaries of the entourage were modest, but Elvis covered almost every other expense as well, from cars to dentists and even houses.

In Hollywood, Elvis dressed his entourage in dark suits and sunglasses, giving rise to the name 'Memphis Mafia'. He gave them all briefcases so they looked like they were doing something. Gene Smith carried a hairbrush and a doorknob around in his.

Elvis designed his TCB lightning bolt logo in the 60s and put the logo on his entourage's jackets and jewellery. It stands for 'Taking Care of Business in a flash'. Elvis later made up the 'TLC' insignia for wives and girlfriends – 'Tender Loving Care'.

Elvis's entourage was always on call, whatever the hour. He would wake them up in the middle of the night to play racquetball, have some shooting practice, or even fly to Las Vegas.

Elvis had bracelets made for his inner circle, with their name on top and their nickname underneath. They got together and gave Elvis his own bracelet. The nickname was 'Crazy'.

One Christmas Elvis handed each of his entourage an envelope. Inside were McDonalds 50-cent gift vouchers. After a moment of panic Elvis revealed the joke and gave them the huge bonuses they were all expecting.

One of Elvis's most cherished possessions was a pendant given to him by the Memphis Mafia in 1967. It was a gold 'tree of life' with all their names engraved on it.

By 1976 Red and Sonny West were becoming increasingly erratic bodyguards, preferring to hit first and ask questions later. When they knocked a man out after refusing him admission to a party, the man sued. Vernon fired them, along with another aide, Dave Hebler, and the three vowed to get even. The result – *Elvis: What Happened?* – was a sensational exposé of Elvis's life.

Elvis: What Happened? was published in the summer of 1977. When Elvis saw a copy he cried, 'Those bastards. They're going to finish me.' After his death it sold some three million copies.

Lloyd Shearer interviewed Elvis for *Parade* magazine and asked him why he surrounded himself with men who were in many ways beneath him. 'You can surround yourself with people [who are] your so-called equals, and there can be dissension, there can be jealousy ... I have my own way of learning ... It's more important to try to surround yourself with people who can give you a little happiness.'

HOT DOG

Once Elvis had the money to buy whatever food he wanted, he made up for those hungry childhood years – and then some . . .

Elvis's first solid food was 'goody mush', a porridge made by mashing the inside of a corn bread with a vegetable such as peas.

Baby Elvis also loved 'soaks', corn bread dunked in buttermilk, and later enjoyed this comfort food in his bed at Graceland.

As a youngster, Elvis's meals generally comprised corn bread, fried okra and a mess of greens grown in his Aunt Lillian's 'truck patch'. These would be mustard greens in the spring, and collard or turnip greens in the autumn. Tupelo residents ate their greens with pepper sauce, stored for several months in an old Coca-Cola bottle until hot.

Expensive meat such as steak never made an appearance on the Presley table. Pork chops would be an occasional treat on payday, and Elvis was partial to the odd squirrel that fell foul of Vernon Presley's shotgun.

While Vernon was in prison for forging a cheque, Elvis and Gladys lived mainly on grits and cheese, a basic Southern subsistence dish. They were also entitled to 'commodities', government handouts of basics such as sugar and beans.

Elvis ate grits the Southern way – he made a hole in a mound of grits with the back of a spoon, and filled the hole with margarine.

Elvis didn't like tomato ketchup. When they were on tour, Bill Black's wife Evelyn would smother her chips in ketchup because that was the only way to stop Elvis pinching them.

Elvis's between-shows snack in the early days was chicken soup with crackers.

The newly successful Elvis liked to hire out the fairgrounds after hours in Memphis, where he would indulge in candyfloss, hot dogs and caramel popcorn.

The Gridiron, on what is now Elvis Presley Boulevard in Memphis, was a regular haunt, where Elvis ate Palm Beach burgers washed down with a chocolate shake or a Coke float.

Elvis's dream snack was a fried peanut butter and banana sandwich. (Bananas must be mushed, not sliced.) Just one contains 92% of the recommended daily fat intake for an adult male.

In a Jacksonville hotel Elvis once asked what ice cream was available. On being told there were 28 flavours to choose from, Elvis asked for a scoop each of all 28 – and ate them, too.

Elvis's first meal as Private Presley was fried eggs and sausage. While posted in Germany he grew to love wieners and sauerkraut.

Elvis loved Krystal burgers. Krystal was the McDonalds of the South, and its burgers were square and very small, so you'd order a few at a time. Elvis ate them by the dozen.

At Graceland, Elvis employed several day cooks and a night cook, Pauline Nicholson. Due to Elvis's nocturnal existence, Pauline was usually the busiest. She cooked his green beans very soft and his mashed potatoes very buttery, and she cut up his steak into bite-size pieces for him.

Elvis preferred his drinks in giant gold-plated glasses, with lots of ice chips to chew on.

For breakfast Elvis liked orange juice, a Spanish omelette, a couple of pounds of bacon (burned) and plenty of black coffee.

Elvis hated to see chicken before it was cooked. It reminded him of having to kill and pluck chickens as a child. He hadn't minded chopping off their heads so much, but putting the body into boiling water was 'the most disgusting smell in the whole world'.

Even in the 1960s, Elvis was spending $500 a week on groceries.

In the Elvis Hall of Fame in Gatlinburg, Tennessee, there's a shopping list on display. It lists everything that had to be available for Elvis at all times, every single day, wherever he was. The list includes: pickles, Pepsi, banana pudding, shredded coconut, at least three bottles of milk, fudge cookies, ingredients for meat loaf, and three pieces each of spearmint, doublemint and juicy-fruit chewing gum.

Elvis drank too much Pepsi to buy it from a store – it was delivered in bulk direct to Graceland by the Pepsi distribution lorries.

With each meal, Elvis had a separate bread plate containing half a dozen hot, buttery biscuits – and they had to be hot. The cook would make two batches so none sat around and got cold.

One of Elvis's most common requests at Graceland was what he called 'ugly steak', a top sirloin steak that curled up on frying to look, well, ugly.

Elvis always drank Sealtest buttermilk and Mountain Valley Spring water. He liked his coffee strong and scalding, and his iced tea strong and sweet.

At New Year, Elvis would eat sliced ham with black-eyed peas, an old Southern tradition to bring good luck.

Elvis once ate meat loaf 28 days in a row.

Never one to miss a food opportunity, Elvis even ate snow. On the rare occasions when weather permitted in Memphis, Elvis mixed snow, vanilla extract and sugar together to make snow cream.

Elvis had a refrigerator in his bedroom.

Elvis ate Krispy Kreme doughnuts a box at a time. His favourites were the jam ones.

Elvis had a charge account at Coletta's Italian restaurant in Memphis. He ordered two or three pizzas at a time and particularly liked the barbecue pizza, which was invented at this restaurant.

Elvis once flew his private jet two hours to Denver in the middle of the night for a sandwich. The Fool's Gold was a whole loaf of bread, hollowed out and filled with bacon, peanut butter and jam. It was made at the Colorado Gold Mine Company restaurant and cost $49.95. This nocturnal food flit made No. 5 in Q magazine's 2003 list of the 100 Most Insane Moments in Rock.

Elvis liked to eat food off his girlfriends, mostly whipped cream with some strategically placed slices of kiwi fruit and a chocolate-covered cherry.

Elvis didn't like alcohol much and he hated beer. When he did drink he mostly stuck to margaritas.

Elvis was a diet aficionado and could lose pounds in weight in a very short time. He would take diet pills, or stick for weeks to one food, such as jelly made from sliced bananas and his favourite low-cal drink, Diet Shasta.

Elvis didn't like shrimps, mussels or other 'freaky' seafood. Priscilla once told Andy Warhol that she never ate caviar because Elvis wouldn't let her.

The last meal Elvis ever had was a plate of ice cream and cookies. He ate it in bed at around 3 a.m. on the morning of the day he died.

I GOT A WOMAN

She was the envy of millions, but being married to Elvis was not exactly fairy-tale stuff. Here's the story of Mrs Presley.

Priscilla Beaulieu was born in Brooklyn in 1945. Her father was a US Navy pilot who died when Priscilla was a few months old. Priscilla's mother Ann married Air Force Major Joseph Paul Beaulieu several years later.

When Elvis was in Bad Nauheim, Germany on army service, Priscilla's stepfather was stationed at nearby Wiesbaden. American service families would socialise at the Eagles Club, and it was there that Elvis's friend Currie Grant approached Priscilla and asked her if she'd like to meet Elvis Presley. She was fourteen years old.

Priscilla first met Elvis in the autumn of 1959 at 14 Goethestrasse in Bad Nauheim. When Elvis saw Priscilla his first words to her were, 'Well, what have we here?' During the evening Elvis sang at the piano and ate bacon sandwiches until it was time for Priscilla to go home.

Elvis told Charlie Hodge, 'Did you see the bone structure in her face? It's like the woman I've been looking for all my life.' Elvis knew she was young, and he thought he could 'train' her to be just the way he wanted her to be.

For his remaining few months in Germany, Elvis saw Priscilla constantly, pouring his heart out to her about his career, his mother and his feelings of loneliness. He won the trust of her parents via his army uniform and his Southern politeness.

The first Christmas gift Elvis gave Priscilla was a gold watch set with diamonds. She gave him a set of bongo drums that she could only just afford, only finding later that he already had a cupboardful of bongos in the basement.

The night before leaving Germany, Elvis told Priscilla for the first time that he loved her. She begged him to consummate their love, but he wouldn't – in fact he would not do so until their wedding night seven years later.

When Elvis left Germany Priscilla accompanied him to the airport, where he handed her his combat jacket and sergeant's stripes and waved to her from the steps of the plane.

Priscilla didn't see Elvis again until the summer of 1962, when she came to visit him in Bel Air. Her parents had finally agreed to her going for two weeks, provided she was constantly chaperoned and wrote home daily.

After two days in Bel Air, Elvis took Priscilla to Las Vegas. In accordance with the rules laid down by her father, she pre-wrote a load of postcards to be sent, with a Bel Air postmark, to her parents every day.

In Vegas, Elvis bought Priscilla a load of dresses and got the hotel hairdresser to do her hair and make-up in the beehive panda look that Elvis liked. When Priscilla flew home a few days later, she was still made up Elvis-style. At the airport, her mother shoved a mirror at her and wouldn't speak to her until she'd washed her face.

Priscilla finally got to Memphis for Christmas 1962. Vernon brought her from the airport but Elvis insisted that he be the one to drive her through the gates of Graceland. Priscilla met all the usual entourage, then promptly spent two days asleep after taking two of Elvis's horse pills.

Elvis gave Priscilla a poodle for Christmas, which she named Honey.

In 1963 Priscilla moved to America for good. She enrolled at the Immaculate Conception in Memphis, an all-girls high school. She was supposed to be living with Vernon and his new wife Dee, but was soon fully installed at Graceland.

Late nights and partying played havoc with Priscilla's studying. She passed her algebra exam by persuading the student next to her to show her the answers in return for an invitation to Graceland.

Elvis gave Priscilla a red Corvair, her first car, as a graduation present. In order not to disrupt proceedings, he waited outside during the graduation ceremony, signing autographs for a bevy of excited nuns.

Priscilla stopped taking Elvis's pills after a pillow fight got out of hand and Elvis gave her a black eye by mistake. She picked up the nickname 'Toughie'. Elvis declined to give up pills with her.

Priscilla believed that Elvis could cure her headaches simply by touching her temples.

Elvis finally proposed to Priscilla shortly before Christmas 1966. He gave her an engagement ring made of a 3½-carat diamond encircled by a detachable row of smaller diamonds. He had always told her that he'd know when the time was right.

Elvis and Priscilla were married on 1 May 1967 at the Aladdin Hotel in Las Vegas. Colonel Parker had arranged it and after an eight-minute ceremony the happy couple were rushed out for a photo session and press conference.

After the wedding the Presleys returned to their rented house in Palm Springs aboard Frank Sinatra's Learjet. Elvis carried Priscilla across the threshold singing 'The Hawaiian Wedding Song'.

Priscilla became pregnant straight away. By eating one meal a day and snacking on hard-boiled eggs, she put on only a few pounds and never needed to buy maternity clothes.

Priscilla's baby shower was organised by Nancy Sinatra.

When Priscilla went into labour, decoy drivers left Graceland first to lure away the press. Before leaving the house Priscilla did her full hair and make-up, and later at the hospital she asked permission to keep on her double set of false eyelashes.

Lisa Marie was born at Baptist Memorial Hospital on 1 February 1968. Elvis was overjoyed, and particularly delighted that his new daughter had a shock of jet-black hair.

Elvis didn't make love to Priscilla for many months after their daughter's birth, and even when he did, the passion was waning. Priscilla started taking private dancing lessons and had a brief affair with her dance teacher.

In 1972 Priscilla began an affair with Mike Stone. He was a karate expert who met Elvis backstage one day when he was acting as bodyguard to a record producer. Priscilla had recently taken up martial arts and Elvis had suggested that she train with Stone.

When Priscilla announced to Elvis that she was leaving him, she told him she was finding her own life for the first time. They divorced on 9 October 1973, at the Santa Monica courthouse in California. They agreed to share custody of Lisa Marie. The split was amicable; in fact, Elvis never bothered to pick up his copy of the divorce papers.

After Elvis's death, Priscilla and Lisa Marie went to view him in the coffin and placed a silver bracelet depicting a mother and child's clasped hands on his right wrist.

I WANT YOU, I NEED YOU, I LOVE YOU

From the avalanche of hits that came pouring out of Elvis, these are the ten essential pop tracks.

'Too Much', 1956

Available on *30 #1 Hits*

A great rhythm and a 'flip flip' make this a marvellous throw-away number for Elvis. Scotty Moore's guitar solo was so improvised that he never managed to reproduce it.

'Don't Be Cruel', 1956

Available on *30 #1 Hits*

Rock chick Suzi Quatro's favourite Elvis song, and one of Elvis's favourites too – although when he heard Jackie Wilson sing it in Vegas, he preferred Wilson's version: 'Man, I was under the table when he got through singing.'

'All Shook Up', 1957

Available on *30 #1 Hits*

A laid-back song that Elvis just glides his way through. Uh huh huh.

'It's Now Or Never', 1960

Available on *Elvis Is Back*

Elvis does opera – or near enough. He found it hard to hit the final note, but when the engineer suggested splicing the ending on, Elvis said, 'I'm going to do it all the way through, or I'm not going to do it.' He did it.

'Stuck On You', 1960
Available on *Elvis Is Back*
This is sexy, clever and catchy, with plenty of trademark moans and groans. Elvis didn't like it much, but hey, what does he know?

'Such A Night', 1960
Available on *Elvis Is Back*
A fantastic pop song – fast, funny and with a great big whoop of enjoyment at the end.

'Little Sister', 1961
Available on *Something For Everybody*
This is the funky, nasty Elvis on top form. Take four was a master but he liked it so much he sang it over and over for the rest of the night.

'(Marie's The Name Of) His Latest Flame', 1961
Available on *30 #1 Hits*
Elvis was so impatient to sing this that he came in after three bars instead of the conventional four. The result is a fresh, exciting start to a perfect pop hit.

'Good Luck Charm', 1961
Available on *30 #1 Hits*
The sort of song Elvis could do standing on his head, and which he approached with businesslike efficiency. 'If we goof up,' he told the band, 'just keep going.'

'Way Down', 1976
    Available on *Moody Blue*
    Released in the UK just weeks before his death, this was a great
    rocking pop hit to bow out to, with the final deep note taken,
    fittingly, by Elvis's long-time friend and mentor, J.D. Sumner.

IF I CAN DREAM

Some Elvis detractors seem to hold him personally responsible for the segregated nature of the world he grew up in. But this was a man who sang for 'a better land where all our brothers walk hand in hand', and who openly praised his musical heroes of all colours.

In 1956, everything from water fountains to education was segregated; Citizens' Councils posted notices saying, 'Help Save the Youth of America. Don't Buy Negro Records', and people were just starting to hear about a Baptist minister called Martin Luther King.

'The beautiful thing about Elvis was he turned everybody into everybody. It doesn't matter "is the guy black or white" any more, and maybe even *you* can do it; it sparked a dream.' Keith Richards.

When Elvis, Scotty and Bill recorded their very first songs, Bill said, 'They'll run us out of town!' In the early years Elvis was abused as a 'white nigger' and 'nigger trash'. Some radio executives wanted him expelled from country music charts because he sang 'mongrel' music. But Elvis never stopped singing the way he wanted to.

In such a segregated society, Elvis was the first 'crossover' performer, reflected in one of his nicknames, the Hillbilly Cat. In the

1950s, some record companies still had separate 'race' catalogues. Elvis rendered these obsolete.

'Elvis was the perfect one for the "transition" that I wanted to make to help the black person to get a reception and help the white person feel that hey, we got a kinship, especially in the South.' Sam Phillips.

Elvis himself never pretended that he had invented rock'n'roll. 'The coloured folks been singing it and playing it just like I'm doing now, man, for more years than I know ... I got it from them.'

In 1956 Elvis attended the WDIA Goodwill Revue, an annual benefit for needy black children in Memphis. B.B. King, who was there, said that 'for a young white boy to show up at an all-black function took guts'.

'Presley makes no secret of his respect for the work of Negroes, nor of their influence on his own singing. Furthermore, he does not shun them, either in public or private.' *Tan* magazine, 1957.

In June 1956 the black newspaper *Memphis World* reported that Elvis 'cracked Memphis segregation laws' by attending the fairgrounds on what was normally designated 'coloured night'.

Myrna Smith of the Sweet Inspirations recalls that when Elvis played the Houston Astrodome, certain parties told him he should 'leave the black girls'. Elvis promptly insisted that they get star treatment, and they were driven round the Astrodome in an open-top car for all the world to see.

'It is perhaps refreshing to freedom-loving people everywhere to tune in on Southern television broadcasts and see white teenagers dancing to the tunes of Little Richard, Fats Domino, LaVern Baker and, of course, Elvis Presley.' *Associated Negro Press*, 1957.

'[Elvis] dared to do in the light of day what America had been doing in the sneak-thief anonymity of night – he consorted on a human level with blacks.' Eldridge Cleaver, black activist.

Elvis regularly topped rhythm and blues charts in black areas across the US. Black DJ Nat Williams saw him in concert and witnessed 'a thousand black, brown and beige girls [who] took off like scalded cats in the direction of Elvis'.

'He was an integrator. Elvis was a blessing. They wouldn't let black music through. He opened the door for black music.' Little Richard.

On stage in Vegas in 1970, Elvis stopped between songs to say, 'There was a guy that said one time . . . he said, "You never stood in that man's shoes, or saw things through his eyes. Or stood and watched with helpless hands, while the heart inside you dies. So help your brother along the way, no matter where he starts. For the same God that made you made him too. These men with broken hearts."' He then sang 'Walk A Mile In My Shoes'.

'He should be celebrated as one of the first great Southern people who tried to cross all barriers of race and join everyone together.' Tom Petty.

Professor Vernon Chadwick of the University of Mississippi claimed at the Elvis Conference in 1995 that, 'If it weren't for Elvis, millions and millions would still be enslaved in the thinking patterns of the oppressed and culturally colonised.'

Elvis was once accused of having said that all that black people were good for was buying his records and shining his shoes. His response was simple: 'I never said anything like that, and people who know me know I wouldn't have said it.' *Jet* magazine looked into the allegations and dismissed them, concluding, 'To Elvis, people are people, regardless of race, colour or creed.'

'You didn't have to be of any racial persuasion for him to love you.' Myrna Smith.

How did Elvis get so popular in such a hostile world? A teenager's letter to a newspaper of the time explains: 'You adults give us a world of racial unrest and expect us to be like you. We are not going to be led around like sheep.'

'[It's about time] the South produced something besides segregation and discrimination ... and Elvis is perhaps it.' *Tri-State Defender*, 1956.

MARIE'S THE NAME

She was the love of his life, she's filthy rich and she's got his looks. It's tough being Lisa Marie Presley.

Lisa Marie was born on 1 February 1968, nine months to the day after her parents' wedding. The name Marie was chosen in honour of Colonel Parker's wife.

Elvis never called his daughter Lisa unless he was angry with her. Otherwise, it was Buttonhead or Yisa.

Elvis gave his toddler daughter birthday presents such as slot machines, St Bernard puppies and an entire roomful of balloons. At three, she got a mink coat and a diamond ring.

When Lisa Marie was five years old Elvis sang 'The First Time Ever I Saw Your Face' to her at a Las Vegas concert.

One of Lisa Marie's more elaborate gifts was a customised baby-blue golf cart with a rose painted on the side. The last thing she and Elvis did together was take a ride round the grounds in the cart, the evening before he died.

Elvis's will left everything to Lisa Marie (with provisions for Vernon and his grandmother). It was all held in trust until her 25th birthday. On reaching that age, she decided to keep it in trust for another five years.

Threats of kidnapping were made against Lisa Marie throughout her childhood. After the divorce, Priscilla sent her to the Lycée Française in Los Angeles, which was used to famous offspring and had good security systems in place. Priscilla also did a thorough job of keeping her daughter's face out of the media so nobody was entirely sure what she looked like.

Lisa Marie's bedroom upstairs at Graceland is exactly the same as it was when she was a child. She visits the house often – but not during Elvis Week.

Lisa Marie began to abuse drugs in her early teens, but got back on her feet when she joined the Church of Scientology at the age of seventeen. There she met musician Danny Keough, whom she later married. The marriage lasted only six years but they remain close friends. They have two children, Danielle and Benjamin. Danielle has recently made her catwalk debut, at the age of fourteen.

In 1994, Graceland met Neverland when Lisa Marie married Michael Jackson in a secret ceremony in the Dominican Republic. They had met for the first time many years before when Elvis took her to a Jackson Five concert. Lisa Marie was said to be thrilled to find someone so famous that he wouldn't be overwhelmed by her own background. But she soon came to believe she'd just been part of a PR stunt and dumped him in 1996.

Lisa Marie married Elvis fanatic Nicolas Cage on 10 August 2002. In November he filed for divorce. She won't discuss the relationship.

Since her thirtieth birthday in 1998 Lisa Marie has chaired Elvis Presley Enterprises.

Lisa Marie brought out her first album, *To Whom It May Concern*, in 2003. The *Independent* reviewer said, 'While the album could be better, it could have been one hell of a lot worse.'

GOOD ROCKIN' TONIGHT

Given his popularity, Elvis sang surprisingly infrequently on television. But every TV appearance he did make was classic Elvis, from the world-changing performances of the 50s to the Hawaiian extravaganza, watched by the world, in 1973.

Elvis's official TV debut was a live broadcast from the Louisiana Hayride on 5 March 1955. Only viewers in the Shreveport area got to see it.

Elvis's first national TV appearance was at 8 p.m. on Saturday 28 January 1956, on the Dorsey brothers' *Stage Show*. Elvis performed 'Shake, Rattle And Roll/Flip, Flop And Fly' and 'I Got A Woman' live from CBS Studio 50 on 1697 Broadway, New York.

Elvis was unknown outside the South at the time, and the show won just 18% audience share. His stay in New York for that first TV show was the last time he was able to walk around any city freely.

Elvis performed on *Stage Show* five more times, through February and March. He sang his first RCA number, 'Heartbreak Hotel', on his third appearance.

On 3 April 1956 Elvis appeared on *The Milton Berle Show*. The show was broadcast from the deck of the aircraft carrier USS *Hancock*, off San Diego. Elvis was paid $3,000 for his appearance, which included a comic duet with Milton Berle dressed up as Elvis's hick brother, Melvin.

On his 5 June performance on *The Milton Berle Show*, from the NBC Studio in LA, Elvis did his notorious version of 'Hound Dog' with the half-speed ending and the bumps and grinds. Next day, the press was filled with outrage. TV host Steve Allen, who had booked Elvis on his show for 1 July, was put under pressure to cancel after Elvis's 5 June performance. Allen announced that if Elvis appeared he 'will not be allowed any of his offensive tactics'. Elvis ended up dressed in white tie and tails singing 'Hound Dog' in a constrained fashion to a bored basset hound. He earned $5,000 from the show but hated every minute of it. The next day, fans picketed the studio with signs saying: 'We want the gyratin' Elvis'.

Later in the evening of the tie-and-tails show, Elvis was back on TV doing a phone interview on *Hy Gardner Calling*. He spent most of the interview with his eyes shut and told the viewers he was 'all mixed up'.

By autumn 1956 Elvis was the biggest star around. He appeared on *The Ed Sullivan Show* on 9 September and was watched by 43 million people – an 80% audience share, the biggest ever for a variety show at that time.

History's most famous act of censorship – Elvis being filmed from the waist up – actually came into force on his *third* appearance on Ed Sullivan's show, on 6 January 1957. At the end of the show Sullivan told viewers, 'This is a real decent, fine boy ... We've never had a pleasanter experience with a big name than we've had with you.'

Elvis was paid $50,000 for his three appearances with Ed Sullivan, a record sum at the time.

Elvis's return to civilian life was celebrated on 'Frank Sinatra's Welcome Home Party For Elvis Presley'. The one-off special was taped on 26 March 1960, and aired on 12 May. It got a 67% audience share. Elvis, dressed in a perfectly draped tuxedo, sang 'Fame And Fortune' and 'Stuck On You', his new releases. Then he duetted with Sinatra, Elvis singing 'Witchcraft', Frank massacring 'Love Me Tender'. Elvis was paid $125,000 for the show, the highest fee ever then paid for a TV guest appearance.

In 1968, after eight years in the Hollywood wilderness, Elvis made the greatest comeback in show business, with his NBC TV Special, called simply 'Elvis'. It was broadcast on 3 December and gave NBC its biggest ratings for the year. In a press conference before the show, Elvis joked, 'I thought I'd better do it before I get too old.'

The show was sponsored by Singer Sewing Machines for $400,000. Shooting took place from 20–30 June. Elvis slept on a camp bed in the dressing room because the schedule was so intense. The show was a mixture of choreographed, rehearsed production numbers, and intimate sets before a live audience. The 'live' section included a sit-down show with Elvis and his mates jamming and reminiscing. Scotty Moore and D.J. Fontana, Elvis's guitarist and drummer from the early days, were there – the last time they would ever play with Elvis.

This was one of the few occasions when Elvis went against Colonel Parker's wishes. Parker wanted to fill the show with Christmas songs. Elvis knew the show would be make-or-break for him, left out the Christmas stuff and did it raw and passionate, clad mainly in black leather. It succeeded in showing the 'real' Elvis. At one point between songs, for no particular reason, he picked up his microphone stand, brandished it like a harpoon and shouted 'Moby Dick!'

Steve Binder was the show's director. He had recently caused controversy when he directed Petula Clark and Harry Belafonte in TV's first interracial embrace. Binder asked vocal arranger Earl Brown to write a closing song that would sum up what Elvis was all about. Brown worked through the night and created 'If I Can Dream'. Elvis sang it as if his life depended on it, in a white Edwardian suit in front of giant red letters spelling out his name.

The *Los Angeles Times* review sneered, 'I don't think many viewers care to see singers sweat on TV.' But of course it was the sweat, and nerves, the *realness* of it that everybody liked. Jon Landau, who became Bruce Springsteen's manager, said of the show, 'There is something magical in watching a man who had lost himself find his way home.'

On 14 January 1973, Elvis performed his live spectacular 'Aloha From Hawaii Via Satellite' – the first live global show ever broadcast. 'Aloha From Hawaii' took place at the Honolulu International Convention Center and was a benefit to raise money for the Kui Lee cancer fund. Kui Lee was a Hawaiian songwriter who penned one of Elvis's favourites, 'I'll Remember You'. The show's main sponsor was the not-very-cool Chicken of the Sea tuna company.

Producer Marty Pasetta was nervous about telling Elvis his ideas for the show, especially when Elvis's entourage all turned up and put their guns on the table. But he plucked up courage and told Elvis, 'You've got to lose weight, because you're too fat.' Elvis burst out laughing, gave Pasetta a hug, and said he'd do whatever Marty wanted. Elvis went on a crash diet and lost 25 pounds for the show. The diet apparently comprised a limit of 500 calories a day of dried food, plus daily injections of urine from a pregnant woman.

Elvis recorded a dry run on 12 January. After watching the tapes he decided he didn't like his hair and had it restyled for the main event. During the dress rehearsal in front of an audience, the night before the live broadcast, Elvis threw his $10,000 cape and belt to the crowd. Tailors worked overnight to make replacements. Elvis threw those away too.

The stage set reflected the worldwide nature of the show, with Elvis's name in different scripts spelt out in flashing lights. The show was broadcast live at 12.30 a.m. to catch the peak TV slot in Japan, where the build-up to the show was declared Elvis Presley Week. It then went out slightly later elsewhere. In Japan, 40% of viewers saw it. In the Phillipines the figure was 90%, and 50% in the USA. Worldwide, over one billion people in forty countries watched the show – more than had watched Neil Armstrong walk on the moon.

Elvis was supremely polished and professional in his Hawaii performance. But, whether it was sheer nerves, or the weight of his fame, or something else, there was a sadness and detachment about him in this show that was oddly mesmerising.

TOO MUCH MONKEY BUSINESS

You wouldn't necessarily have Elvis down as an animal lover, but his choice of 'Old Shep' for his first public performance turns out to have been quite fitting.

As a small boy Elvis played with a couple of scruffy dogs that he named Woodlawn and Muffy Dee.

Elvis once had a dog with hair sticking out all over, which he called Spontaneous Combustion.

Elvis bought a spider monkey, Jayhew, which he kept in a custom-built cage in the house on Audubon Drive. Elvis bought him because he couldn't bear to see him in the small cage that had been his home. The monkey's new home was filled with every toy Elvis could find, but it still had an unfortunate self-abuse habit.

The first horse Elvis owned was a golden palomino, which he bought in 1967. A powerful, attention-loving creature that had been trained for shows, he was the perfect horse for Elvis. He called it Rising Sun and its stable was, of course, called the House of the Rising Sun. Elvis soon bought horses for all his friends and their wives.

Elvis also bought Bear, a black Tennessee walking horse. He would dress in full regalia and put on a high-stepping show for the fans at the gate. After Bear died he bought Ebony's Double. This walking horse eventually retired from championships in 1983, after a performance to a medley of Elvis music.

Elvis owned two Great Danes named Snoopy and Brutus. Brutus played the part of the dog Albert in Elvis's film *Live a Little, Love a Little*.

Ever the corny punster, Elvis named another horse Mare Ingram, after one Mr Ingram who was then mayor of Memphis.

In the 1970s a chow called Getlow used to sleep on the end of Elvis's bed. When the dog developed kidney problems Elvis spent a fortune flying it to the New England Institute of Comparative Medicine for (unsuccessful) treatment.

Australian fans sent Elvis two wallabies, which later went to Memphis Zoo. Colonel Parker wrote Elvis a letter saying, 'It is impossible to housebreak a wallaby since it does not have any natural sanitation instinct.'

Elvis's most famous pet was probably Scatter, the chimpanzee he bought in 1961. Scatter had been a TV star and was unfazed by all Elvis's women – in fact he hugely enjoyed looking up their skirts, which Elvis found hilarious.

Ducks, chickens, mynah birds and a turkey called Bowtie could all be found at Graceland. Elvis also had some peacocks, but they were dispatched to Memphis Zoo after one of them scratched his Rolls-Royce while studying its own reflection.

HOW GREAT THOU ART

Elvis was very religious, from his gospel beginnings to his later, increasingly desperate, search for meaning. Although Elvis seemed to give up on himself, he never gave up on God.

In his copy of *Through The Eyes Of The Masters: Meditations And Portraits*, Elvis wrote, 'God loves you but he loves you best when you sing.'

Both in Tupelo and in Memphis, the Presleys attended the revivalist First Assembly of God church. Elvis was transfixed by its fire-and-brimstone preaching and rousing spiritual singing.

More than anything else, Elvis was upset by condemnation from religious leaders. He believed that the talent he had, and the way he portrayed it, came from God. In 1956 he told *True Story*, 'My voice is God's will, not mine.'

Early girlfriend June Juanico gave Elvis a copy of Kahlil Gibran's *The Prophet*. Elvis read it over and over throughout his life and called it his 'unwinder'.

Elvis liked to relax after shows by singing gospel songs into the night. He said, 'It more or less puts your mind at ease; it does mine.' Sometimes he got his backing singers to sing from the shower stall of his hotel suite, to get the 'reverb'.

Elvis first met Larry Geller in April 1964, when Geller came to Elvis's house in Bel Air as a replacement hairdresser. Geller told Elvis that he was interested in spirituality and the meaning of life. Elvis broke down and told him he was trying to understand why he was Elvis Presley. Geller quit his job and returned the next day with the books Elvis was crying out to read. Geller had a huge influence on Elvis, which neither the Memphis Mafia nor Colonel Parker was happy about. He was eventually eased out of the inner circle, and Priscilla persuaded Elvis to burn a lot of his spiritual books. But Elvis still sought out Geller, and an answer.

Among Elvis's favourite books were *Autobiography Of A Yogi*, *Beyond The Himalayas* and *The Impersonal Life*, which he gave to all of his friends to read. He also read *Leaves Of Gold*, which contained different people's philosophies on life and death.

One of Elvis's favourite biblical quotations was: 'And ye shall know the truth, and the truth shall make you free' (St John, chapter 8, verse 32).

Although a Christian, Elvis wore a chai, a Jewish symbol of life, around his neck. In 1964 he changed his mother's headstone to one with a cross on one side and the Star of David on the other. He also came up with a design for a watch that would alternate the cross and the Star of David on its face, as a symbol of unity. As he put it, 'I don't want to miss out on heaven on a technicality.'

In March 1965, while driving to Los Angeles, Elvis saw a cloud formation in the desert that resembled first the face of Stalin, then that of Jesus. This gave him a newfound serenity and he told Larry Geller that he wanted to become a monk. The fact that he had been awake for almost two days at this point may or may not have had something to do with it.

Elvis became involved with the Self-Realization Fellowship in 1965, and spent considerable time at the group's Lake Shrine retreat in Pacific Palisades. Sri Daya Mata, the group's leader, would be involved in Elvis's spiritual journey for the rest of his life. Through his studies with Sri Daya Mata, Elvis became fascinated by the life of Indian holy man Yogananda, whose body remained undecomposed for over twenty days after his death. This 'higher state of consciousness' was what Elvis hoped to achieve.

During a performance at Notre Dame, a group of girls sitting across one row stood up and unfurled a banner saying: 'Elvis, you're the King'. Elvis stopped singing and said, 'No, Jesus Christ is the King.' The girls all sat down again rather sheepishly.

At one point Elvis got interested in Cheiro's *Book Of Numbers*, which defines people's characteristics by their birth date. He was a number eight – which Elvis defined to a friend as someone who is intensely lonely at heart, hides their feelings and does just what they want.

Elvis once claimed he could see angels dancing in the water sprinklers of the Bel Air Country Club.

Elvis copied out these words from *The Kahlil Gibran Diary For 1973*: 'If I wasn't tough I wouldn't be here. If I wasn't gentle I wouldn't deserve to be here.'

In 1976 Elvis considered singing solely gospel music, but friend and preacher Rex Humbard told him he was 'tilling the soil for others to sow the seed'.

When Elvis died various books were lying near his body, including *The Scientific Search For The Face Of Jesus*, about the Turin shroud, and *Sex And Psychic Energy*.

Elvis was obsessed with his mortality. He once took Priscilla to the Memphis morgue (his fame got him into all sorts of places) to show her the bodies. He wanted to show her how fleeting it all was, and how everything could be over in a moment.

'Help me, Lord, to know the right thing.' Note in Elvis's hotel suite, Las Vegas, 1976.

I WANT YOU, I NEED YOU, I LOVE YOU

You don't have to be religious to be bowled over by Elvis's gospel voice – it's the musical equivalent of Durham Cathedral. These ten essential gospel songs, with the exception of 'If I Can Dream', are all available on *Amazing Grace*.

'Take My Hand, Precious Lord', 1957
Elvis sings this, like all his gospel songs, with complete sincerity. A beautiful, moving rendition.

'Milky White Way', 1960
Never mind the lyrics – just listen to the voice. You'll believe in angels by the end of this song.

'Run On', 1966
This a joyful, energetic, you're-going-to-hell piece of gospel music. Elvis is clearly loving it, and it's mesmerising from the first 'hmmm'.

'Stand By Me', 1966
All of Elvis's spiritual exploration of the 60s can be heard in this song. He sounds as if he's desperate for somebody to answer.

'Where Could I Go But To The Lord', 1966
Elvis and Vernon used to sing this often at home. A slow, bluesy spiritual with lots of finger-snapping, jazzy piano, and a big dose of soul.

'Farther Along', 1966
Elvis's voice cracks a couple of times during this song, as he sings of death that takes our loved ones. He's never sounded more vulnerable than this.

'If I Can Dream', 1968
Available on *Memories*
Not strictly gospel, but there's a definite spiritual feel to the passion with which Elvis sings for a better future. Written specially for him, Elvis felt so strongly about this song that he recorded it curled up in the foetal position on the studio floor.

'Lead Me, Guide Me', 1971
Who could produce a gospel song this beautiful just minutes after doing a karate demonstration that resulted in a gun getting lodged in someone's guitar? Only Elvis.

'An Evening Prayer', 1971
Elvis gives due respect to his heroine Mahalia Jackson with this cover. It's intense, highly operatic and very personal.

'If That Isn't Love', 1973
The most hardened atheist will be beating down the church door after hearing this. Elvis's passion and conviction give you goosebumps.

RAISED ON ROCK

Elvis's influence on the musicians who followed him cannot be underestimated. Much of the music we listen to now, we listen to because of Elvis.

'You have no idea how great he is, really you don't. You have no comprehension – it's absolutely impossible. I can't tell you why he's so great, but he is. He's sensational.' Phil Spector.

'Nothing really affected me until I heard Elvis. If there hadn't been Elvis, there wouldn't have been the Beatles.' John Lennon.

Bob Dylan, who fell into deep depression when Elvis died, once declared, 'Hearing Elvis's voice for the first time was like busting out of jail.'

When Bruce Springsteen saw Elvis on TV he went straight out and bought himself a guitar. The first thing he did was stand in front of a mirror with it and try to move like Elvis. 'I remember right from that time, I looked at [my mother] and said, "I wanna be just like that".'

'It was like the world went from black-and-white to technicolour.' Keith Richards.

'Without Elvis Presley none of us could have made it.' Buddy Holly.

John Lennon had a picture of Elvis on his bedroom wall. His Aunt Mimi once said to him, 'Elvis Presley's all very well, John, but not for breakfast, tea and dinner.'

Johnny Hallyday is France's very own Elvis. He once told a music journalist that all he ever wanted to be was a cross between Elvis Presley and James Dean. Although generally unknown and unappreciated outside France, Hallyday has sold 80 million records. The leather-clad pensioner is on his fifth wife and still going strong.

To celebrate being named as European City of Culture for 2008, Liverpool has opened a permanent exhibition called Fingerprints of Elvis. The words of John Lennon are inscribed at the site: 'Before there was Elvis, there was nothing.'

'I was a real little toddler when I first heard "Hound Dog". I learned to play drums listening to him – beating on tin cans to his records.' Mick Fleetwood.

Ray Manzareck of the Doors saw Elvis on TV as a child: 'The darkest, meanest, most dangerous white man ever to be on television. [It was] one of the transcendent moments of my life, altered my destiny – OK, that's what I want, white guys can do rock'n'roll too.'

'Ask anyone. If it hadn't been for Elvis, I don't know where popular music would be. He was the one that started it all off, and he was definitely the start of it for me.' Elton John.

After meeting k.d. lang backstage at a concert, Madonna announced, 'Elvis is alive – and she's beautiful.'

'I picked up the guitar because I wanted to be like Elvis Presley.' Paul Simon.

David Bowie's first live performance, aged eleven, was an Elvis impersonation for an audience of boy scouts in Bromley. Years later, Bowie would paint Elvis's lightning bolt logo onto his face for the cover of his album *Aladdin Sane*. Ziggy Stardust concerts often closed with the song *Rock'n'Roll Suicide*, for which Bowie changed into an Elvis-style jump suit, before departing the stage to the announcement, 'David Bowie has left the building.'

'People like myself, Mick Jagger and all the others only really followed in his footsteps.' Rod Stewart.

Nick Cave sang 'In The Ghetto' on the Bad Seeds' album, *From Her To Eternity*.

'He was the firstest with the mostest.' Roy Orbison.

Chris Isaac, whose hair and singing style owe much to Elvis, sang 'Blue Moon' at an Elvis tribute concert in Memphis in 1994.

'As soon as I heard "Hound Dog" I got myself a quiff. I must have looked a pretty strange six-year-old kid.' Alice Cooper.

Cliff Richard was known as the British Elvis. In 1963 *Billboard* even named Cliff the world's No. 1 artist, with Presley trailing in second place. The lip-curling, bequiffed singer launched his pop career in 1958 with 'Move It'. And, like Elvis, his early live performances were also deemed dangerously sexy . . .

'Elvis is my man.' Janis Joplin.

'They didn't make a mistake when they called him the King.' B.B. King.

Bono said, 'Elvis woke up my heart.' He wrote his song 'American David' about Elvis. In U2 concerts, Bono draws on the ghost of Elvis for two of his favourite 'characters': lounge singer MacPhisto who sings 'Can't Help Falling In Love'; and The Fly, a tragic figure based on the Elvis who sat in Graceland shooting out TV sets, nearing meltdown.

'Elvis created the template for what the celebrity rock-star persona had to live up to.' Marilyn Manson.

'I never wanted to become like Elvis . . . I don't want to become a fat, rich, sick, reclusive rock star. I want to continue as I've always done.' Johnny Rotten. Mr Rotten recently appeared in *I'm A [D-list] Celebrity, Get Me Out Of Here*.

'Everyone in rock'n'roll, including myself, was touched by his spirit. I was, and always will be, a fan.' Bryan Ferry.

MONEY HONEY

As fast as Elvis earned it – and boy did he earn it – he spent it.

'He was generous beyond his means. He gave away most everything he had.' Joe Moscheo of the Imperials.

Variety's banner headline on 24 October 1956 was simply: 'Elvis: A millionaire in one year'.

Elvis's main bank was the National Bank of Commerce in Memphis. He liked to have a million dollars in his current account at all times. Beyond that, he took no interest in his finances whatsoever.

When he joined the army, Elvis was already earning some $100,000 a month. His two-year service cost the US an estimated $500,000 in tax revenue.

For much of his career, Elvis lost 80 cents of every dollar he earned, to the taxman and Colonel Parker. He once said, 'I'd rather pay my taxes than worry about them.'

When the Lansky brothers saw a young man staring through the window at the clothes in their store, one of them went outside and asked if he wanted to buy something. Elvis replied that he couldn't afford to buy anything that day, but one day he would buy them out. The Lanskys replied, don't buy us out, just buy from us. And Elvis did, for the rest of his life.

For Christmas 1954 Elvis went to Harry Levitch Jewellers on South Main Street and bought his mother an electric mixer. A few days later he returned and bought another one – she'd liked it so much he wanted her to have one at each end of the kitchen.

In 1957 Elvis bought 1,400 tickets for the E.H. Crump Memorial Football Game for the Blind, an annual charity game in Memphis. The tickets were a gift for all the pupils of Humes High School.

Elvis had TCB pendants made up and gave them to his closest friends. The jeweller Lowell Hays, who made most of them, said, 'When Elvis gave me my necklace, it was like being knighted.' Costume designer Bill Belew's reaction on receiving one was, 'Oh shit, I really have come into it now.'

In the two weeks after he bought his Circle G ranch, Elvis spent over $100,000 on trailers, horseboxes, fencing and ranch equipment. Vernon begged him to stop but he said, 'I'm having fun, Daddy, for the first time in ages.'

Elvis gave Sammy Davis Jr a $30,000 ring, explaining, 'Nobody thinks of giving a rich man anything.'

Always a fan of new gadgets, Elvis bought a mobile phone for his Stutz Blackhawk. It cost him $1,467.

In 1975 Elvis bought two planes. He paid a million dollars for a Convair 880 jet formerly owned by Delta Airlines, and named it *Lisa Marie*. He put the TCB lightning bolt logo on the tail fin, and did up the rooms in leather, suede and the obligatory gold. A crew of four was on call to fly it at all times. Then he bought a Lockheed Jetstar for business flights. He named it *Hound Dog II*.

Hound Dog II's crew was captained by the aptly named Milo High. A small plaque in the plane is inscribed, 'O God. Thy sky is so great and my plane is so small.'

Once Elvis gave J.D. Sumner a $40,000 gift of a gold and diamond ring, on stage, as a thank you for entertaining the audience while he went for a loo break.

Elvis rarely carried money with him – one of his Memphis Mafia would generally be on hand to do the paying.

During the 70s, Lowell Hays sold some $700,000 worth of jewellery to Elvis. Elvis would call him at any hour of the day or night and buy items on a whim. Hays even went on tour with him. Elvis designed some rings himself, including the square ring studded with diamonds and black sapphires that he wore on his last tour.

Elvis bought a new tour bus for J.D. Sumner and the Stamps, on condition that he could drive it. When the vehicle was delivered J.D. brought it to Graceland and Elvis took the gleaming new bus careering down Elvis Presley Boulevard and round a field.

Elvis bought houses for masses of people, including Linda Thompson, her parents and her brother Sam. Jerry Schilling's mother had died when he was a baby, so Elvis bought him a house, saying, 'I wanted to be the one to give you a home.' And when he bought a house for his cook, Mary Jenkins, he gave the estate agent Portia Fisher – and her mother – a car each to say thank you for closing the deal.

Elvis gave huge amounts of money to charity, especially local causes. Many Memphis groups received donations along with his standard letter: 'Gentlemen, Please accept the enclosed check, as a small contribution to the great work your organisation is doing for our city and country. Yours very sincerely, Elvis Presley.'

Elvis once bought an entire stand of melons from a small boy on the roadside.

In 1973 Elvis asked Donnie Sumner, J.D.'s nephew, to form a singing group, Voice, to follow Elvis round his houses and basically be 'on call' for singing gospel music any time of day or night. It cost him $100,000 a year.

Elvis was a huge fan of Muhammad Ali and gave him a $10,000 robe with 'The People's Champion' embroidered on the back. Ali wore it for a fight that he then lost – he never wore it again.

When singer Jackie Wilson suffered a stroke, Elvis sent his wife a cheque for $30,000.

The largest single contribution ever made to the Motion Picture Relief Fund was $50,000, from Elvis.

Elvis bought a black dune buggy from Liberace and rode on the dunes when he was living in Palm Springs.

Elvis spent $100,000 on a trip to Hawaii in 1977. He took thirty friends with him. Elvis told friend Larry Geller, 'What profiteth it to gain the world if you couldn't share your good fortune with your friends?' It was to be the last holiday Elvis ever took.

'When he started he couldn't spell Tennessee. Now he owns it.' Bob Hope.

Elvis once told producer Felton Jarvis that he sometimes gave people things to show them that life would be the same after they got it as it was before.

It keeps right on a' hurtin'

For the medically minded, here's a look at Elvis's physical imperfections (yes, girls, there were some).

Elvis suffered terrible acne as a teenager and when he was in Germany he fell for the quackery of Laurenz Johannes Griessel Landau, a South African masseur who claimed to be able to give Elvis 'new skin'. Several times a week for six weeks, Lawrence treated Elvis's face and gave him a massage. The arrangement ended abruptly when Lawrence started making homosexual advances.

Elvis once broke his little finger playing football. He told a reporter at the hospital, 'No, it won't affect my strumming a guitar.' He broke another finger, years later, doing karate.

From an early age, Elvis suffered greatly from insomnia, and also had action nightmares where he would wander around and punch out at imagined opponents.

Elvis suffered frequently with throat problems, a weakness that he wasn't above exploiting. Hearing one day that he'd gone down with severe tonsillitis and fever while out on army manoeuvres, Priscilla rushed to hospital, where she found Elvis tucked up cosily in bed and warming up his thermometer with a lighted match.

One of Elvis's problems was inherited – a ganglionic fold. This is a disease whereby the colon is not as efficient as it should be. To make matters worse, Elvis used too many laxatives, so his whole digestive system was weak, causing a distended abdomen and considerable pain.

Elvis inhaled a porcelain dental cap during the filming of *Jailhouse Rock* and had to go to hospital to have it removed from his lung. This involved manhandling his vocal cords – a job thankfully done by a competent surgeon.

Besides the drugs (see 'Too Much') Elvis often suffered from sheer exhaustion brought about by his phenomenal touring schedule.

Towards the end of his life Elvis was often hospitalised. He went to Baptist Memorial Hospital in Memphis, where he had the windows of his room covered in tin foil, like at home. The nurses used to connect his TV to the nursery so he could see the newborn babies.

Elvis wasn't a huge fan of washing at the best of times. In his final years, when his grip on reality was loose to say the least, he took a Swedish herbal mixture that was supposed to achieve inner and, he hoped, outer cleanliness without soap and water.

During a plane journey in 1971, Elvis wrote out a TCB oath. As well as pledging to strive for sharper skills and greater respect towards others, he also sought, rather woefully, 'freedom from constipation'.

In the 70s Elvis suffered from iritis and a secondary form of glaucoma, which was aggravated by hair dye mixing with his sweat and running into his eyes. He once had to have an injection of cortisone directly into the eyeball, without anaesthetic, which he became rather proud of and would describe to anyone who could bear to listen.

In 1975 Elvis had cosmetic surgery around his eyes, despite everyone telling him he didn't need it. His cousin Billy Smith thought it had ruined him, as it took the sleepy droop away.

At his death Elvis's heart was found to be up to 50% larger than normal. This is a classic symptom of heart failure and would explain the dizziness, shortness of breath and high blood pressure that plagued Elvis in his final years.

GIRLS! GIRLS! GIRLS!

Women fell over themselves to get to Elvis. Here are a few of the ones who made it.

Right from the off, Elvis liked his women. His Aunt Lillian recalled that he would always rather have a bunch of girls around him than a bunch of boys.

Early girlfriend Dixie Locke went to the school prom with Elvis. They dated for a long time and even discussed marriage. She liked him because, while the other boys were just mini-versions of their fathers, Elvis was different. The first time her family met him, her uncle offered him two dollars to get his hair cut.

Biloxi beauty June Juanico first met Elvis in June 1955, after he spotted her in the audience at a concert. They had an incredibly innocent, 1950s relationship. On the one occasion when they got close to full-blown sex, they were 'saved' by the arrival of Elvis's mother.

While Elvis was away in Hollywood with the starlets, June became engaged to a local man. In March 1957 Elvis telegrammed for June to meet him at Union Station in New Orleans, where he would be changing trains. When he saw her he told her he had a huge surprise for her, which she had to come and see. She told him she couldn't come; she loved him, but she was getting married. The next day June read in the paper: 'Elvis buys Graceland'.

Elvis dated the actress Natalie Wood, whom he met in Hollywood in 1956. Natalie, who was used to hanging around with the James Dean crowd, found non-drinking, non-swearing Elvis refreshingly conventional, like the high-school date she'd never had. She visited Elvis at his home in Audubon Drive, Memphis, and was astounded at the throng around the house. In her years in Hollywood with all the stars, she'd never seen anything like it.

Anita Wood was a Memphis DJ and hostess of TV's *Top Ten Dance Party* when she met Elvis. They were pretty serious for a long time, and she wrote him dozens of letters while he was in Germany (which Priscilla wasn't overjoyed to find). She also released a record on the Sun label, called 'I'll Wait Forever'. She was going to have to.

Debra Paget was Elvis's co-star in *Love Me Tender* and accounts vary as to whether or not they really got it on. She dug her claws in years later, though, saying she'd turned him down because he was 'too much backwoods, if you know what I mean'.

On vacation in Vegas, Elvis briefly dated Tempest Storm, a stripper who brought out his romantic side – he once said to her, 'I'm as horny as a billy goat in a pepper patch. I'll race you to the bed.'

Dolores Hart was Elvis's co-star in *Loving You* and *King Creole*. He called her 'Hot lips' after acting a kissing scene in sweltering New Orleans. She said that he was charming but unrefined, like a young animal. Shortly afterwards, Dolores entered a convent.

Within days of arriving in Germany, Elvis began dating a local girl called Margit Buergin, whom he had met in the park. She had been strategically placed there by a press photographer, who predicted that Elvis would like her as she resembled Brigitte Bardot. In a letter to his friend Alan Fortas, Elvis described his relationship with Margit as 'Grind City'. Margit became an overnight star in Germany, but after a few months Elvis dumped her when she posed for pin-up pictures in a US forces magazine.

Elisabeth Stefaniak was a young fan who met Elvis at the cinema and became his live-in secretary at Bad Nauheim. She fell in love with him and often shared his bed – but not, to her regret, exclusively. She later married Elvis's army friend Rex Mansfield.

While in Germany, Elvis also dated 18-year-old starlet Vera Tschechowa. Her fans wrote complaining that Elvis was an uncouth American who was unworthy of her. She seemed to agree, being particularly put off by his friends, but Elvis did make an effort. He once hired out a theatre where she was performing in a play, and he, Red West and Lamar Fike sat baffled while the actors gave their all in German to an audience of three.

On army leave in Paris, Elvis stayed at the Hotel Prince de Galles, on Avenue George V. A waiter described the girls as going in and out of Monsieur Presley's suite like a door revolving. One evening the manager of the Lido nightclub had to phone Elvis to ask for his girls back so they could start the show – the entire chorus line was in his hotel room.

Barbara Leigh, who was best known for her portrayal of cult figure Vampirella, dated Elvis for two years – at the same time as she was dating Steve McQueen.

Ann-Margret was Elvis's co-star in *Viva Las Vegas*. She had actually been nicknamed the 'female Elvis' by the press. They fell heavily in love and Elvis's friends thought she was great for him

– unlike most women, she wasn't in awe of him. Elvis was so smitten that he would actually go to her house – normally, the women had to come to him.

Ann-Margret made the mistake of speaking about their relationship to the press, and Elvis cut off the affair completely. But despite everything their feelings for each other remained. Years later, in Vegas, Ann-Margret was in the audience for one of Elvis's shows. He held her in the spotlight, saying, 'Put the light on her, man. I want to look at her.'

When they met Elvis, the Beatles – the *Beatles* – were astounded at the number of women around him.

Elvis had a lot of paternity suits filed against him, the first being in 1956 from a girl in Ohio. None of them ever won.

Elvis briefly dated the actress Joan Blackman. He wooed her by driving up to her on the Paramount lot and yelling, 'Hey, you, c'mere!'

Elvis and Nancy Sinatra were almost lovers but not quite. Longstanding friends, they starred together in *Speedway* and roughhoused around in their trailers, but the one time he kissed her he quickly pulled away and apologised. She later recalled, 'I thought I was going to die.'

Elvis had a relationship with Kathy Westmoreland, the soprano he always introduced on stage as 'the little girl with the beautiful high voice'. He read to her and recited poetry. One day he told everyone she was still a virgin and couldn't understand why this embarrassed her, telling her how proud he was because not many girls would have held out for so long. She only 'held out' for a few more hours after that.

Elvis dated fellow Memphian Cybill Shepherd for a short while. She first met him in the cinema and smelled him before she saw him – not a recognisable perfume, just the aura of Elvis entering the room. The affair is best remembered for her revelation that burgers weren't the only thing that Elvis liked to eat.

Elvis met Linda Thompson in 1972 when George Klein invited her to a late-night movie screening in Memphis. She had just become Miss Tennessee and completely bowled Elvis over. For a year, she was with him 24 hours a day. Linda finally left Elvis in November 1976. She loved him and had cared for him completely through his worst times, but, without the knowledge that he only had a few more months to live, she just couldn't cope with it any more.

Elvis met Ginger Alden in November 1976. She was Miss Mid-South and looked uncannily like Priscilla. They argued a lot but Elvis soon proposed marriage to her, and although she was completely out of her depth, she agreed. It was Ginger who found Elvis's body.

I WANT YOU, I NEED YOU, I LOVE YOU

Joe Cocker called Elvis the greatest white blues singer in the world. These ten essential blues tracks prove it.

'Heartbreak Hotel', 1956
Available on *Elvis Presley*
So famous it's hard for us to imagine the shock this grim suicidal ditty caused on its release. Elvis never doubted it – he said it would be his first RCA hit before he even recorded it.

'How's The World Treating You', 1956
Available on *The King Of Rock'n'Roll: The Complete 50s Masters*
You may want to hang yourself from the nearest tree by the end of this song, but it's worth it. The 21-year-old Elvis sings as if he has 100 years of pain on his shoulders.

'So Glad You're Mine', 1956
Available on *The King Of Rock'n'Roll*
Elvis shows off his vocal skills with great aplomb here. The thumping bass complements his 'oo-whee' superbly.

'One Night', 1957
Available on *The King of Rock'n'Roll*
Even toned down from its original 'One Night Of Sin', this intense, raunchy track reminds us why Elvis had polite society sweating all those years ago.

'Santa Claus Is Back In Town', 1957

Available on *Christmas Peace*

Santa in a big black Cadillac, coming down your chimney tonight? This song is simply *rude*, and Elvis is clearly loving it.

'Reconsider Baby', 1960

Available on *Elvis Is Back*

Only a night owl like Elvis could record a song like this, this well, at seven in the morning. Boots Randolph's sax solo, the first on a Presley record, contributes to this being Elvis's greatest ever blues number.

'Fever', 1960

Available on *Elvis Is Back*

With a perfect, sultry vocal and a timely shake of the congas, this is one hot, hot song and a deserving classic.

'Like A Baby', 1960

Available on *Elvis Is Back*

Oozing saxophone and a slow, raunchy lyric put this up there with the greats. What did the army *do* to Elvis?

'After Loving You', 1969

Available on *From Elvis In Memphis*

Elvis finally gets his teeth into a song he'd loved for years, and makes it his own.

'I'll Hold You In My Heart', 1969

Available on *From Elvis In Memphis*

Elvis blues up an old country song and gets so lost in it that despite the band stopping twice, he just keeps right on singing. A one-take wonder.

A CANE AND A HIGH STARCHED COLLAR

Half the time, Elvis's 1970s stage outfits were actually a step down from his daywear. Move over, P Diddy – Elvis was the king of bling when you were still in nappies.

The first costume that Bill Belew designed for Elvis was the black leather number for the 1968 TV special. He went on to design all of Elvis's stage outfits and became his personal fashion designer. Elvis spent up to $15,000 a month on 'home' clothes.

Bill Belew said Elvis was 'a great person to dress. He had a terrific build.'

One of Elvis's favourite coats was made of red wool with a high collar and a detachable black fur cape. He was also partial to a brown velvet trouser suit with a polka-dot lining and additional cape. These were all for casual wear.

Another favourite ensemble was a black and white fur coat, white velvet trousers and a velvet hat. Don't try this at home.

When Bill Belew designed a suit for Elvis, he would use the same patterned silk to make both the shirt and the lining of the jacket.

For a while Elvis went through a puff-sleeved shirt phase and ordered dozens. He finally got bored of them and went back to his usual understated self.

One of Elvis's most famous pieces of jewellery from the 70s is his TCB ring. It was made of gold, black onyx and 16 carats in diamonds.

Elvis went through an unfortunate phase of carrying a cane around with him. The handle of the cane was in the shape of a lion's head, with red rubies for eyes. With that and the cape, he was like one of the backing musicians for Count Dracula.

When he 'dropped in' on President Nixon in 1972, Elvis was wearing jewelled aviator glasses, a caped Edwardian jacket with brass buttons, a velvet tunic and trousers, and his gold belt from Las Vegas. He wasn't arrested.

Elvis decided that the karate uniform, the 'ghi', was what he needed for his return to live performances. Bill Belew made a number of ghis, both black and white, and ordered a macramé sash, interwoven with karate symbols, from a Hawaiian–Japanese martial arts lover.

Elvis's stage outfits started off relatively simple but Bill Belew made them more and more elaborate after studying the reactions of the fans.

Belew came up with the idea of the Napoleonic stand-up collar because Elvis thought his neck was too long. It also throws attention onto the face.

Elvis generally preferred black jump suits, but white worked better under the stage lights.

The jump suits were constructed by IC Costume Company of Santa Monica Boulevard, Hollywood. They were made from

Italian-wool gabardine, which is what ice skaters wear for maximum flexibility. It took ten people up to four days to make one. The stones generally came from Austria or Czechoslovakia and were selected by Bill Belew on his buying trips to Paris.

Elvis approved most of Belew's designs by sight, and would rarely tolerate having a fitting, so the seamstresses had to size the outfits with visual judgment and a heavy dose of tact.

The jump suits are all known by name: Red Dragon, Blue Aztec, Mad Tiger, Mexican Sundial and Burning Love, to name but a few.

Designer Gene Doucette worked alongside Bill Belew in the creation of Elvis's jump suits. His embroidery work so impressed other stars that he went on to design for the likes of Cher, Dolly Parton and Diana Ross.

Before he got into capes, Elvis favoured fringes on his jump suits. Perhaps they reminded him of one of his nattier home outfits, an American Indian leather and long-fringe combo – not advisable near revolving doors.

The earlier suits weighed around 25lb, but later ones, with the cape, were as much as 75lb. It was Elvis's idea to add the capes and belts to his stage outfits, as he enjoyed wearing such items off stage.

Elvis's jump-suited, theatrical appearance was described by *Variety* as 'the essence of kabuki drama'.

The iconic eagle jump suit from the Hawaii show was Elvis's idea. He wanted something quintessentially American. Bill Belew originally made a calf-length cape for the show but it was just too heavy to wear, so he made a waist-length version instead.

By 1975 Elvis started to phase out capes in his stage shows because they were easy to grab hold of and he was nearly dragged into the audience several times by fans.

Elvis ordered silk scarves in dozens to give to fans during shows. He also took to wearing sticking plasters on his fingers to stop his rings being wrenched off as he handed the scarves out.

'If the songs don't go over, we can always do a medley of costumes.' Elvis, backstage on opening night, Las Vegas, 1970.

I'M MOVIN' ON

For two years in the 50s, and for much of the 70s, Elvis pretty much lived life on the road. Here's a look at the locations and the logistics of Elvis live on stage.

Elvis's first advertised performance was at the Overton Park Shell in Memphis on 30 July 1954. Slim Whitman, singing 'Indian Love Call', was the star of the show. Elvis, his name misspelled 'Ellis', was at the bottom of the playbill.

Between July 1954 and November 1957, Elvis had 420 show bookings all over the Southern states – and they're just the ones for which there is a written record. He often made two or three appearances at each booking.

Elvis, Scotty and Bill originally called themselves the Blue Moon Boys, after 'Blue Moon Of Kentucky', which was the B-side to 'That's All Right'.

Through the latter half of 1954 the trio played regularly as the intermission band at the Eagle's Nest on Lamar Avenue, Memphis. Teenagers would come for the intermission and leave before the headline band came on stage.

In September 1954 Elvis performed from the back of a truck for the opening of the Lamar Airways Shopping Center in Memphis.

Elvis performed at the Grand Ole Opry in Nashville in October 1954. The notoriously conservative audience for the Opry gave Elvis a tepid reception and he never went back.

On the road, Elvis carried the tools of his trade in his breast pocket – a pen for signing autographs, and a comb for doing his hair.

Elvis made his debut at the Louisiana Hayride on 16 October 1954. He was paid $18. Elvis stood out a mile as Hayride acts generally dressed in cowboy outfits. The audience didn't know what to make of him at first, but it wasn't long before teenagers had taken over the audience and he had to be the closing act because nobody could go on after him. His payment later rose to $200 a show.

Drummer D.J. Fontana joined the outfit after Elvis's early appearances at the Hayride.

Elvis continued to perform almost every Saturday at the Louisiana Hayride until 31 March 1956. His contract ran until September so Colonel Parker bought him out for $10,000 and the promise of a farewell concert. This concert took place in the Louisiana Fair Grounds on 15 December 1956. Film director Hal Kanter was there: 'If I came to scoff, I went away a prophet.'

'People said we did so many wild things . . . I wish we'd have done all those things but we didn't have time; we were right back in that car the minute the show was over, moving another five hundred miles.' D.J. Fontana.

In May 1955, Elvis was a 'Special Added Attraction' on Hank Snow's All Star Jamboree, and did a three-week tour to new territory – Florida and the southeast.

By the end of 1955, big-name artists refused to go on a bill with Elvis.

Touring took its toll, even on a young Elvis. In February 1956 he collapsed from exhaustion after a show. The doctor told him to slow down. He didn't. When he walked off stage, he would be completely soaked in sweat.

After a show in Amarillo on 13 April 1956, Elvis, Scotty and Bill took a small charter plane headed for Nashville. On the way the engine died and the plane started to drop. The pilot switched fuel tanks and the engine restarted, but for years afterwards Elvis would take buses and trains to avoid flying.

On 4 July 1956, just three days after he had to wear a tie and tails on *The Steve Allen Show*, Elvis gave a rapturous homecoming concert at Russwood Park in Memphis, where he announced, 'Those people in New York are not gonna change me none. I'm gonna show you what the real Elvis is like tonight.'

On 29 September 1956 Elvis returned to his birthplace to perform at the Tupelo Fairgrounds, where he had stood on a chair and sung 'Old Shep' eleven years earlier. Despite the presence of a hundred police and National Guardsmen, Elvis had to stop the show and ask the crowd to calm down before someone got hurt.

In 1960 Elvis returned from the army. On 25 February 1961 (Elvis Presley Day in Tennessee), he played two benefit shows at the Ellis Auditorium in Memphis. A month later he played another benefit, this time in Hawaii for the USS *Arizona* memorial appeal. He would not set foot on stage again until 1968.

Elvis decided to return to live performance after the success of his TV special. He told interviewers again and again that he simply missed the excitement and the closeness of a live audience.

While performing in Las Vegas, Elvis was tipped off that there was a woman in the audience who was planning to shoot him. Elvis packed a gun in his boot and FBI agents mingled in the audience. Nothing happened, but from then on Elvis took security very seriously on his tours and would often enter buildings through kitchens, back elevators and side exits. His entourage were given photo ID cards and anybody without one would not be allowed backstage.

After Vegas (see 'Viva Las Vegas'), Elvis began his return to touring with a six-show run at the Houston Astrodome in February 1970. It was a sell-out and made over one million dollars in three nights. Despite the nerve-wracking size of the venue (Elvis described it as a 'goddamn ocean') he was on top form and provoked mass hysteria.

From 1970 to his death Elvis played around 800 shows.

Elvis performed in all but nine US states: Alaska, Idaho, Montana, Wyoming, North Dakota, Delaware, New Jersey, New Hampshire and Vermont. He performed in more towns in Texas than in any other state.

Elvis played around a hundred towns a year, in stints of about three weeks with a different town every night. He rarely saw the arena before he actually came on stage for the performance, so would usually stand for a moment to get his bearings before greeting the crowd.

The 1970s tours were huge and complex operations. Joe Esposito was road manager and there were around a hundred people in each tour group. Stage crew wore blue overalls with 'EP' embroidered in gold letters on the back.

For most of his 70s shows, Elvis's backing musicians were: James Burton on lead guitar; Jerry Scheff on Fender bass; Glen Hardin on piano; Ronnie Tutt on drums; John Wilkinson on rhythm guitar; and the Joe Guercio orchestra.

Elvis wanted all musical spectrums covered, so he blended white gospel quartets (first the Imperials, later the Stamps) with the Sweet Inspirations, who had backed Aretha Franklin.

From 1971 onwards, Elvis used to open his show with Strauss's *Also Sprach Zarathustra*, best known for its use in *2001: A Space Odyssey* but originally written as a musical tribute to Nietzsche's writings on the human superman. It's not known whether Elvis was aware of this . . .

On stage, Elvis used to drink Mountain Valley Spring water or Gatorade to quench his thirst.

In the 70s Elvis put loads of karate moves into his performance. Drummer Ronnie Tutt actually took martial arts classes to help him anticipate Elvis's moves and drum accordingly. He had to watch Elvis all the time because the singer was so unpredictable.

In June 1972 Elvis went to New York and became the first performer ever to sell out four successive concerts at Madison Square Garden. It was his first time in New York since 1956, and his first stage performance in the city. Eager ticket buyers included George Harrison, John Lennon and Bob Dylan.

Reviewers were astounded. The *New York Times* said that when Elvis came onto the stage 'he looked like a prince from another planet'. *Billboard* said, 'Elvis has transcended the exasperating constrictions of time and place.'

In 1972 MGM made *Elvis On Tour*, which followed Presley as he crossed the States giving performances. It won a Golden Globe for Best Documentary – thanks in part, no doubt, to the montage supervisor, one Martin Scorsese.

From 1974 onwards Elvis spent much of his concerts giving rambling monologues. He once gave a bemused audience a lengthy lecture on the history, philosophy and technique of karate.

Elvis liked to introduce himself as other people – often Wayne Newton, Johnny Cash or Glen Campbell, or occasionally, Bill Cosby.

When Elvis opened the newly built Rushmore Plaza Civic Center in Rapid City, South Dakota, he was presented on stage with a medallion of life from the Sioux Nation.

Given Elvis's poor health, remarkably few shows were actually cancelled. In 1973–4, seventeen shows were cancelled. The worst year was 1975 with almost two entire Vegas fortnights called off. Elvis made every date in 1976, and cancelled three in 1977.

When Elvis performed in Houston in August 1976, members of the audience were crying for the wrong reasons. Elvis came on stage ninety minutes late, he was bloated, his skin was yellow, and his words were slurred. The critic at the *Houston Post* wrote, 'Elvis Presley has been breaking hearts for more than twenty years now, and, Saturday afternoon . . . he broke mine.'

In March 1977, on stage in Alexandria, Louisiana, Elvis changed the words of 'Can't Help Falling In Love' to: 'Wise men know, when it's time to go . . . ' The next night, he was too ill to go on.

Elvis was filmed on tour again, in June 1977. Why Colonel Parker thought this was a good idea remains unfathomable. CBS aired the film in October of that year, and revealed a desperately ill man crying out for help. Elvis Presley Enterprises no longer allows this programme to be aired or sold in its entirety.

Elvis's final performance was on 26 June 1977 at the Market Square Arena in Indianapolis. It was his best show in a long time, longer than usual, with some strong singing. He brought Vernon on stage, introduced friends in the audience, and prowled the stage as its rightful owner.

Not even death can stop Elvis from movin' on. The multimedia extravaganza *Elvis In Concert* features footage of Elvis on a 20-foot video screen, accompanied by the very same musicians and singers who were with him during his life. It was first staged at the Mid-South Coliseum in Memphis on the twentieth anniversary of Elvis's death and was the Coliseum's largest grossing event ever. The show has played over seventy concerts throughout the US, Europe, Asia and Australia. Typical audience members include Sandra Clarkson of Ohio, who sits with a life-size cardboard cutout of Elvis and proclaims proudly, 'I saw him live once, but dead for the fourth time.' Owen Evans from Wales says simply, 'It doesn't change anything. He's still alive!'

THAT'S SOMEONE YOU'LL NEVER FORGET

You get to meet all sorts when you're Elvis Presley. Here are a few of his more famous acquaintances.

In December 1956 Elvis dropped in at Sun Studio to find Jerry Lee Lewis, Carl Perkins and Johnny Cash inside. An impromptu jam session started, which Sam Phillips secretly recorded. It became known as the Million Dollar Quartet. Twenty years later, Jerry Lee Lewis was arrested after crashing into the gates of Graceland, drunk and in possession of a loaded pistol.

During the filming of *King Creole*, Elvis was having lunch with co-star Jan Shepard when Marlon Brando came along and sat directly behind him. Shepard suggested that Elvis go and talk to his hero. Elvis looked into his bacon sandwich and said, 'No, no, no, no, I can't do that.' But Brando was peeking over at Elvis, too, and finally both men shook hands and talked. After lunch Elvis was bowled over with excitement and kept repeating Brando's name to himself in disbelief.

Elvis first met Tom Jones at the Paramount Studios in LA in 1965. Elvis came walking out of his prop helicopter singing Jones's hit 'With These Hands'. Jones later said he couldn't believe Elvis had heard of him, let alone knew the song. The two became very good friends. When Jones was in Elvis's audience once, Elvis introduced him as 'one of the most fantastic performers I've ever seen'. He told Jones that it was seeing him on stage that had given him the confidence to go back to live shows.

One night in Las Vegas Elvis was ushered backstage to meet Barbra Streisand. She started making sarcastic remarks about his outfit, so he told her she was the ugliest star in Hollywood. They both burst out laughing and struck up a friendship from there.

Elvis met Sammy Davis Jr on the set of *Loving You*. Years later Stanley Kramer approached the two men with a film script about two prisoners who escape, chained together. They were both very keen to do it, but Colonel Parker said some of Elvis's fans wouldn't want to see Elvis chained to a black person. Elvis cried when he told Sammy Davis that he couldn't do the movie.

Bill Medley of the Righteous Brothers was another great friend. Once, in Vegas, Elvis took it upon himself to walk right across the stage in the middle of Bill's afternoon show. Then a minute later he walked right back again. By this time the crowd was going crazy. When he did the same thing again at the packed evening show, Bill Medley said to the audience, 'I don't know who he is, but he's now starting to piss me off.'

Elvis admired Dean Martin and took on some of his vocal style, such as the slurring of notes and the general humorous approach to a song. In 1960 Elvis was photographed alongside Shirley MacLaine, helping Martin to cut his birthday cake. Once, when Dino was in Elvis's Vegas audience, Elvis sang 'Everybody Loves Somebody' as a tribute to him.

Elvis and Muhammad Ali were huge fans of each other. When Elvis told Ali once that he'd like to do boxing, Ali told him, 'No, you're too pretty. You do the singing; I'll do the boxing.'

When Elvis met Jackie Wilson, Wilson showed him the secret of his profuse sweating on stage, which women apparently loved – it was salt tablets and a lot of water. Elvis took it up as a quick and incredibly unhealthy weight-loss technique.

Elvis first met James Brown in LA in 1966. Brown had tried to phone Elvis on several occasions, but Elvis had always been in bed. When Brown finally met him, he said, 'Man, Elvis, you sure do sleep a lot.' Brown sometimes visited Graceland, where he and Elvis would sit in the music room together and sing gospel songs. When Elvis died James Brown asked for, and got, time alone with the body.

Life in Graceland could sometimes be a bit isolating. When introduced to Eric Clapton, Elvis apparently asked, 'And what do you do?'

In August 1965 Elvis invited the Beatles to his home in Bel Air. While Brian Epstein and Colonel Parker played roulette, the boys played a little pool and did some jamming with Elvis. John Lennon later said, 'The only person that we wanted to meet in the USA was Elvis Presley. We can't tell you what a thrill that was.' But the Beatles' press officer remarked that he thought Elvis was 'a boring old fart'.

In December 1970, Elvis turned up at the White House out of the blue and asked to see President Nixon. Sure enough, he was soon ushered into the Oval Office, where he gave Nixon a World War II pistol and asked if he could have a Narcotics Bureau police badge. Nixon duly gave Elvis the badge and some presidential cuff links for his friends, and had his photo taken with him. The White House does not advise the rest of us to turn up unannounced.

VIVA LAS VEGAS

After a false start in 1956, Vegas embraced Elvis like a long-lost son. It's the glitzy, tacky, trashy town that Elvis was made for.

Elvis's first appearance in Las Vegas was on 23 April 1956. Colonel Parker promoted him as the Atomic Powered Singer and booked him for two weeks at the Venus Room of the New Frontier Hotel.

The wealthy middle-aged gamblers were not impressed. Showbiz newspaper *Variety* quipped: 'For the teenagers he's a whizz. For the average Vegas spender he's a fizz.' Elvis soon decided the only way to survive was to make light of the whole thing – he changed the words of his recent hit to 'heartburn motel' and introduced 'Blue Suede Shoes' as 'Get out of the stables, grandma, you're too old to be horsing around.' But Elvis did get to meet Liberace, who gave him some advice on how to dress to please an audience . . .

After the success of his 1968 TV special, Elvis wanted to return to live performing. Colonel Parker headed straight for the International Hotel (later renamed the Hilton) in Las Vegas. The hotel was newly built and had a record 2,000-capacity show-room. Barbra Streisand went in first and dealt with the teething problems, smoothing the way for Elvis to follow her.

Elvis was paid $400,000 for a four-week run, doing two shows a night. Colonel Parker covered the whole of Vegas in ads for the show. Everywhere you looked, there was Elvis's name. But, as he told the nervous star, they all knew Elvis was in town, but only Elvis could make them buy a ticket. Opening night, 31 July 1969, was an invitation-only show. Everyone from Cary Grant to Sam Phillips was there. As Elvis, dressed in a black karate suit, stepped on stage and grabbed hold of the microphone, he was stopped by a roar from the audience. He was getting a standing ovation just for being there. For the second time in his life, Elvis was back.

Rolling Stone magazine called Elvis 'supernatural, his own resurrection'.

In Las Vegas, hotel entertainment facilities are budgeted to operate at a loss, in the expectation that the money will be recouped at the gaming tables. Elvis Presley's was the first show in the history of Vegas to earn a profit. In 1970 the International Hotel gave Elvis a gold belt adorned with the words 'Elvis: World's Championship Attendance Record'.

From 1970 onwards Elvis performed twice a year in Vegas: a fortnight in January/February and again in August/September.

Elvis's rehearsals and spectacular performance in Vegas in 1970 were preserved for posterity in the film *Elvis: That's The Way It Is*. As *Fabulous Las Vegas* magazine neatly summed it up: 'He's all man, top cat, the true king of the musical jungle.'

The Vegas shows were not performed in front of people sitting in rows, like in a theatre, but for people sitting at tables eating dinner. Women would climb over the tables, stepping in meals and knocking over wine glasses, to get to the front. Vegas had never seen anything like it.

From 1969–71 Elvis used the gospel group the Imperials as backing singers. But hardcore gospel fans felt that by appearing in Las Vegas the Imperials had 'gone to the devil', and their gospel bookings started to suffer. They backed out of working with Elvis and were replaced by J.D. Sumner and the Stamps, who would remain with Elvis until the end.

Famous audience members whom Elvis introduced at his Vegas shows include: Buzz Aldrin, Neil Diamond, Telly Savalas, Brenda Lee, Shirley Bassey, Mama Cass, George Hamilton, Fats Domino, Petula Clark, Liza Minnelli, Charlton Heston, Nancy Sinatra, the Righteous Brothers, Roy Orbison, Engelbert Humperdinck and Bob Hope.

The excitement of that incredible comeback couldn't last forever. In December 1976 Elvis announced from stage, 'I hate Las Vegas . . . This is my living, folks, my life.' Preacher Rex Humbard visited Elvis backstage. Elvis held his hand and wept for a long time.

I WANT YOU, I NEED YOU, I LOVE YOU

Elvis was in love with his audiences. Their presence could lift his singing to even greater heights – or give him an excuse to have some fun with a song. Here are ten essential live performances.

'Polk Salad Annie', 1970

Available on *That's The Way It Is*

The ultimate live performance, from the drawling introductory speech to the hyperactive climax. In this recording Elvis is at his physical peak and still in love with his job. It really doesn't get any better than this.

'Bridge Over Troubled Water', 1970

Available on *That's The Way It Is*

This version of the Simon and Garfunkel song is classic 70s Elvis – passionate, personal, and highly dramatic. Guitarist Jerry Scheff liked this best of all Elvis's performances.

'I Just Can't Help Believin'', 1970

Available on *That's The Way It Is*

Elvis was so concerned about this song that Charlie Hodge had the lyric sheet on stage with him. He needn't have bothered. A sublime performance, enhanced by Elvis's urges to the backing singers to 'Sing the song, baby, one more time'. This is actress Jane Horrocks' favourite Elvis song.

'You've Lost That Lovin' Feelin'', 1970
Available on *That's The Way It Is*
'Listen to me talking to you' – Elvis leaves the Righteous Brothers in the dust with this superbly OTT performance.

'I Can't Stop Loving You', 1970
Available on *On Stage*
A great belting song that Elvis has a lot of fun with, dragging out his last 'yesterday' while those drums keep rolling.

'Never Been To Spain', 1972
Available on *Burning Love*
Elvis starts this off slow and raunchy and builds to a rousing ending, which seems particularly heartfelt since he never did go to Spain – or anywhere else much – himself.

'Suspicious Minds', 1972
Available on *An Afternoon In The Garden*
A classic Elvis song becomes a classic one-act drama in his live shows. He draws out the ending, fills it with karate moves, and generally has a ball.

'What Now My Love', 1973
Available on *Aloha From Hawaii*
This is so controlled, you just know that when he lets rip at the end, it's going to blow you away, and it does. 'I feel the world closing in on me' are words that seem torn from his soul.

'An American Trilogy', 1973
Available on *Aloha From Hawaii*
This combination of 'Dixie', 'All My Trials' and 'Battle Hymn Of The Republic' was always guaranteed to bring the house

down. At the Hawaii show it's tinged with an extra weight of emotion that makes it all the greater.

'How Great Thou Art', 1974
Available on *Amazing Grace*
This won a Grammy for best inspirational performance, and it's not hard to see why. When Elvis cries, 'Oh, my God,' he sounds as if he's face to face with Him, pleading for his life.

TOO MUCH

Elvis was an obsessive insomniac, a pressured star to whom nobody ever said no. The last person who should ever have taken a small white pick-me-up one chilly day in Germany.

'Elvis was an extremist in all that he did.' Jerry Schilling.

Elvis had always had trouble sleeping, which was exacerbated when he had to make the switch from his nocturnal existence to army hours. When Gladys died his insomnia got even worse, and he was prescribed sleeping pills.

Out in Germany, a sergeant introduced Elvis to pills that would keep him going on manoeuvres. Within weeks, Elvis was paying an army pharmacist $100 a week for a constant supply of amphetamines. Thus began the seesaw of uppers and downers that would come to dominate Elvis's life.

Elvis was an amateur medic and kept the *Physician's Desk Reference* by his bed. This superficial medical knowledge was enough to convince Elvis that he knew what he was doing when it came to prescription drugs.

Elvis had medicines sent to Graceland from many different cities. To increase the quantities he could get hold of he filled out prescriptions in the names of other people in the house – even his own daughter. By the end, Elvis's drug tolerance was so high that just one of the doses he took would have killed a non-drug-user.

Out in Hollywood, the entire Elvis entourage would take pills just to keep up with each other. In those days, half of the pills weren't even regarded as drugs – doctors routinely prescribed tablets such as Dexedrine to actresses, just to help them stay thin.

In the 60s, Elvis and Priscilla tried marijuana a few times. Neither particularly liked it. To Priscilla's knowledge, Elvis only tried LSD once. After spending some time studying leaves and hearing them breathing, Elvis decided to go back to his usual stuff.

Elvis first met Dr George Nichopoulos in 1967, when his usual doctor was not available. Dr Nick, as Elvis called him, became Elvis's personal physician and chief prescriber. Elvis later paid him $800 a day to accompany him on tour.

Elvis's drug addiction inevitably altered his personality. He was by nature a typical creative type, used to both euphoria and despair, but the drugs magnified this swing and worsened his temper as well. In his last years he suffered weeks-long depressions where he would hardly leave his room.

Elvis was treated for a strained back in 1973 by a Californian doctor. He was given multiple injections of Novocaine, Demerol and steroids, and by the time he came back to Memphis he was addicted to Demerol. By the end he would be injecting it between his toes.

As a result of his sedatives Elvis would frequently fall asleep and choke on his food. Linda Thompson, his girlfriend from 1972 to 1976, lost count of the number of times she had to put her fingers down his throat to save his life.

When he was touring, Elvis would arrive in a new town, take pills to go to sleep, then be roused a couple of hours before the show and take pills to wake him up. After the show, he would take pills to get to sleep again.

Elvis was so immune to ordinary painkillers that he took Dilaudid, usually reserved for cancer patients in cases of extreme suffering.

In 1974, after collapsing in Louisiana, Elvis was admitted to the Baptist Memorial Hospital in Memphis where Vernon put him into a detox programme. When the doctors took him off his sleeping pills they assumed he would eventually go to sleep naturally. After Elvis spent four days awake, the doctors gave in and gave him a sleeping shot.

Elvis's nurse Tish Henley lived in at Graceland and administered packets of drugs to Elvis at 'safe' intervals. By the end of his life his immunity to the drugs grew so great that he sometimes needed three packets to get to sleep.

John O'Grady was an LA policeman and a friend of Elvis. He believed that Elvis was prescribed more drugs than anybody he had seen in 32 years of working in drug enforcement.

A reviewer at a concert in 1976 watched Elvis sing 'And now the end is near' in 'My Way' and wrote, 'It was like witnessing a chilling prophecy.'

Dr Nick prescribed Elvis a total of 4,097 tablets in 1975, 6,111 tablets in 1976, and 8;805 tablets up to August 1977. This did not include the drugs that Elvis got from other doctors.

The lab results from Elvis's autopsy showed that he had fourteen drugs in his system. The pathologists were in no doubt that the cause of death was polypharmacy: having too many different drugs in the system at once.

In 1981 Dr Nick went on trial on ten counts of overprescribing to patients. Two of those named were Elvis and Jerry Lee Lewis. The defence argued that Dr Nick was doing what he had to do, both to support habits and to try to get the dosage down. He was cleared of all charges.

Linda Thompson once asked Elvis what he thought his biggest character flaw was. 'I'm self-destructive,' he replied. 'I recognise it, but there's not a lot I can do about it.'

ANYTHING THAT'S PART OF YOU

The merchandising industry was practically invented for Elvis –
he's the one to blame for all those annoying things in your cereal
packets.

An average day on eBay offers some 8,000 Elvis items in over
1,500 categories.

In 1956 Colonel Parker signed a merchandising deal with Hank
Saperstein. They came up with 72 different Elvis products,
including lunch boxes, stuffed dolls, trading cards and a plastic
guitar. The products made $22 million in six months.

Cosmetic items included lipstick – 'Keep me always on your lips'
– and 'Teddy Bear' perfume. Girls also bought Elvis dog tags, like
the nametags worn by soldiers, with his army number on.

Colonel Parker brought out 'I Like Elvis' badges, based on the 'I
Like Ike' Eisenhower campaign slogan. Never one to miss a
money-making opportunity, he also brought out the Yiddish 'Oy
Gevalt Elvis' and even 'I Hate Elvis'.

Tom Petty and the Heartbreakers used to while away the time on
their tour bus with a 'Best of Elvis' deck of playing cards.

The Elvis Presley Autograph Model record player was finished in
blue denim with Elvis's name stamped on the top – and gave
away eight free records with each purchase.

Art Garfunkel once gave Paul Simon a birthday present of a magic wand filled with hearts, stars, records, musical notes, a pink Cadillac, and a tiny gold lamé Elvis.

Stand aside, Ken – 1997 saw the launch of a two-doll gift set, Barbie Loves Elvis.

Elvisopoly – an Elvis version of Monopoly – was released in 2002, the 25th anniversary of his death.

According to the *Chicago Tribune*, an Internet bidder recently paid $115,000 for a small jar containing some locks of Elvis's hair.

The best-selling items at the Graceland Outlet Store on Elvis Presley Boulevard are any T-shirts, mugs and shot glasses decorated with a picture of Elvis or Graceland.

South America recently got its first Elvis store, the Elvis Shop Argentina in Buenos Aires. Fans in that country can buy a 50s compilation album called *Elvis La Pelvis*.

Butterfield & Butterfield held its first all-Elvis auction in 1994, in – of course – Las Vegas. Actor John Corbett bought Elvis's birth certificate for $68,500, and his American Express card for $41,400.

In October 1999 Elvis Presley Enterprises held an auction of items from its own archives. This was to raise money for Presley Place, a homeless project organised by the Elvis Presley Charitable Foundation. Among the lots were Elvis's 1956 Lincoln Continental, a handgun, his army fatigues with the 'Presley' pocket patch and his prescription sunglasses. The

Lincoln fetched $250,000; Elvis's 1955 RCA contract sold for $65,000.

Joni Mabe from Georgia tours the USA with her 'Travelling Panoramic Encyclopaedia of Everything Elvis'. Her collection contains a toenail from the carpet in the Jungle Room, which is called the 'Maybe Elvis Toenail', and the wart that Elvis had removed from his right wrist in the late 1950s.

A letter from Elvis to Anita Wood, written in 1958 while he was serving in the army, was sold at auction in London in 2001, for £14,100. The letter ended, 'Please don't let anyone read this.'

In 1954 Elvis went to the OK Houck Music Shop in Memphis and traded in the guitar he'd got for his eleventh birthday for a new one. A Seattle businessman paid almost $200,000 for this guitar in 1993. He called it 'the Holy Grail of rock'n'roll'. Elvis watched as the salesman at OK Houck threw the old guitar, the first Elvis ever owned and therefore priceless, in the dustbin.

An Elvis signature on a Las Vegas menu can fetch $1,000. A Humes High School yearbook signed by Elvis is worth $4,000. A 1960s vinyl collection of 33 RCA Compact Singles is worth $12,000.

Impersonator Anthony Ciaglia once paid $8,500 for one of Elvis's shirts. A price worth paying – he'd been roused from a coma by Elvis's music many years before.

In January 2004, a US company called Master Tape Collection upset a lot of people when it claimed to have the original tape from Elvis's 1954 Sun sessions. The tape was apparently too fragile to be played so it had been cut into 5cm pieces and mounted on plaques, on sale for $495 each. Rock critic Dave Marsh said, 'Either they're destroying history or this is a fraud. If it isn't valuable, why are they selling it? And if it is valuable, why are they destroying it?'

Among recent additions to the official Elvis merchandise available are a watch that plays 'Can't Help Falling In Love', and a replica Crown Electric work shirt.

2004 sees the launch of Elvis Presley Collector's Series Wine, from Graceland Cellars. An assortment of wines has been expertly selected to suit all tastes and budgets, and there's a nice picture of Elvis on the labels. Elvis didn't like wine much . . .

Mr Songman

In the end, it's all about the music, and the music just keeps on playing.

Elvis has sold over one billion records and has received more gold and platinum discs than any other artist.

Elvis's first US No. 1 was his very first single with RCA in 1956, 'Heartbreak Hotel'. His latest was 'A Little Less Conversation' in 2002.

Elvis's first UK No. 1 was 'All Shook Up' in 1957. His latest, and nineteenth No 1, was 'A Little Less Conversation' in 2002. 'Jailhouse Rock', 'It's Now Or Never' and 'A Little Less Conversation' all went straight in at No. 1.

Elvis was the first artist to amass over one million US advance orders for a single with 'Love Me Tender' – a gold record before it was even released.

Elvis became the first person ever to succeed himself at No. 1 when 'Love Me Tender' replaced 'Hound Dog' at the top of the US charts.

His biggest-selling single of all time was 'It's Now Or Never'. It sold 1,210,000 copies in the UK alone.

'Wooden Heart' spent the longest time in the UK chart – a massive 27 weeks.

The soundtrack to *Blue Hawaii* was the best-selling Elvis album in his lifetime.

The *ELV1S: 30 #1 Hits* CD has sold 10 million units so far, topping the charts in 26 countries, including Indonesia, the United Arab Emirates and Chile.

According to Guinness's *British Hit Singles*, Elvis has appeared in 1,193 of the weekly charts since they started recording these things in 1952. This remains an unbeaten achievement.

In 2003 *Q* magazine named 'That's All Right' as the most influential song ever recorded.

From 1956 to 1962, Elvis made 31 of RCA's 39 million-selling singles.

Elvis's first recording session for RCA was on 10 January 1956, two days after his 21st birthday. Elvis told producer Steve Scholes, 'Don't make me stand still. If I can't move, I can't sing.' He played guitar until his fingers bled – and he jumped about so much that he ripped his trousers. Guitarist Chet Atkins from RCA called his wife to come down to the studio, because he'd never seen anything like it.

In that first session Elvis recorded 'I Got A Woman' and 'Heartbreak Hotel'. When RCA heard the results they told Steve Scholes there was nothing worth releasing, and to get back to the studio. They only put out 'Heartbreak Hotel' for want of anything better.

'Heartbreak Hotel' was released on 27 January 1956. It sold two million copies, broke all records and became the first song to top all three US charts – country and western, rhythm and blues, and pop.

Right from Elvis's first song with them, RCA had to use the pressing plants of other record labels to keep up with the demand.

Elvis took much longer than was normal at the time to record a song – he would do as many as forty takes then choose one take from memory. And nothing was ever written out in the recording studios – the arrangements just came along as Elvis tried things out. He was effectively his own producer, right from his very first session.

Elvis's first album, called simply *Elvis Presley*, contained cuts from the recent RCA sessions and some unreleased Sun sides. The album sold 300,000 copies, was the first album to make a million dollars, and was the first rock'n'roll album to reach No. 1 – where it stayed for ten weeks.

The album's cover photo of Elvis, mouth open in mid-song, was taken at the Fort Homer Hesterly Armory in Tampa on 8 May 1955. The unposed, tonsil-revealing, monochrome photo, combined with the green and pink lettering of Elvis's name, made an album cover unlike any seen before.

Songwriting duo Leiber and Stoller wrote many hits for Elvis, including 'Don't' and 'Love Me'. They were initially wary about meeting him as neither were Elvis fans and they thought he'd be dreadful, but they were won over by his encyclopaedic knowledge of music, and his total dedication in the studio.

RCA were initially against the idea of Elvis singing gospel songs, as they were afraid it would upset his fan base. But Elvis insisted on singing 'Peace In The Valley' for his mother on *The Ed Sullivan Show*, so they brought out an EP of the same name. It was a million-seller and the best-selling gospel EP of all time.

Elvis would signal his opinion of a demo song in a recording session by patting his head if he liked it, or running his finger across his throat if he didn't.

Elvis recorded most of his music as he lived, from dusk until dawn.

After years of singing movie songs, some of which he hated, Elvis recorded his 1968 TV special, poured his soul into 'If I Can Dream' and announced he would never again record a song he didn't believe in. His next album, *From Elvis In Memphis*, was recorded in 1969 at the American Studio and is his finest ever.

The 1970s recording sessions with Elvis are legendary for their guns, costume changes, karate and the odd tantrum, but the musicians who came back again and again clearly thought it was worth it.

Elvis's last-ever recording session in a commercial studio took place at the Stax studio in Memphis in December 1973. It turned out to be a creative tour de force, so Elvis clearly wasn't put off by the widescreen TVs he'd installed for the Monday night football – nor by the 300 hamburgers that he had delivered.

The last album Elvis made in his life was *Moody Blue* in 1976. The album was recorded in the den, now known as the Jungle Room, at Graceland, with a mobile RCA recording unit called 'Big Red' out in the yard.

At the first recording session for *Moody Blue*, Elvis startled the musicians by appearing in his Denver police uniform. He then disappeared at regular intervals to consider ways to dispense vigilante justice to the criminals of Memphis.

The last song Elvis recorded at Graceland was on 31 October 1976. The song? 'He'll Have To Go'.

'Way Down', Elvis's final single, was released just weeks before his death and remained at No. 1 for five weeks in the UK.

After Elvis's death, an RCA pressing plant in England that had been scheduled to close was reactivated for several months to cope with the demand for Elvis records.

In 2001 Elvis was inducted into the Gospel Hall of Fame, thus becoming the first person to enter the gospel, country and rock halls of fame.

The fiftieth anniversary of the recording of 'That's All Right' was 5 July 2004. As part of its yearlong celebrations, Memphis was the focal point for the 'Global Moment in Time' – the simultaneous playing of the song by the world's radio stations.

On 8 January 2004, at a ceremony in Washington, RCA (now part of BMG) and the Recording Industry Association of America announced the results of a full audit of Elvis's record sales. In all, Elvis has accumulated 97 gold records, of which 55 have gone platinum, and 25 multi-platinum; and 51 gold singles, 27 of which are platinum, and 7 multi-platinum.

IT'S OVER

Elvis died on Tuesday 16 August 1977. He was 42 years old.

'I think it's entirely possible to die of a broken heart.' Sam Phillips.

Elvis woke at his usual time, about 4 p.m., on Monday 15 August. He spent the evening watching TV, playing with Lisa Marie and bickering with his fiancée Ginger Alden. He then went off to see his dentist, Lester Hofman, at around 11 p.m. (Hofman was used to these nocturnal visits and drove around in a free Cadillac as a reward for his relaxed surgery hours.)

Elvis got back from the dentist at about 12.30 a.m. As he drove his Stutz Blackhawk through the gates of Graceland, he waved to the fans assembled there, and Robert Call from Indiana took the last photo of Elvis alive.

At 2.15 a.m. Elvis called Dr Nick for some painkillers. Dr Nick prescribed six Dilaudid and Elvis's stepbrother Rick Stanley picked them up from the all-night pharmacy. Elvis also phoned his nurse, Tish Henley, to request Dilaudid on the pretext of Ginger having period pains.

By 4 a.m. Elvis had taken the Dilaudid and wanted to play racquetball, so he, Ginger, and Billy and Jo Smith played for a while. Then Elvis sat at the piano in the racquetball court and sang some songs. The last song he ever sang was 'Blue Eyes Crying In The Rain'.

Elvis went upstairs and took his first packet of sleeping medication. Ginger recalled him asking for another packet at about 8 a.m., which his Aunt Delta Mae brought up to him. Then Ginger fell deeply asleep.

When Ginger woke at 1.30 p.m. Elvis was not by her side, but this was not particularly unusual. She phoned a friend, then her mother, then knocked at Elvis's bathroom door. She got no response.

Ginger opened the door to find Elvis lying face down on the floor with his knees tucked underneath him. He was wearing only his pyjama trousers, pulled down; his tongue was hanging out of his mouth and his eyes were open. His face was bloated and his body was cold.

The ambulance was called at 2.30 p.m. The caller simply said that someone at 3764 Elvis Presley Boulevard was having trouble breathing. When the paramedics came into the bathroom the body they found was so discoloured that they thought it was the body of a black person. They took Elvis to hospital, trying to revive him all the way, even though rigor mortis had already set in. Elvis was pronounced dead from the hospital an hour later.

An autopsy was undertaken immediately. At 8 p.m. Dr Francisco, chief medical examiner for Shelby county, announced to the press, 'The cause of death is cardiac arrhythmia, due to undetermined heartbeat ... There is no evidence of chronic use of drugs whatsoever.' This extraordinary announcement was made without the agreement of all the medics present and without the autopsy even being finished.

Among the messages of condolences that Vernon received were telegrams from Johnny Cash ('We share your grief'), B.B. King ('... the loss of one of the world's greatest musicians and humanitarians') and Little Richard ('Words are inadequate to express the shock I feel').

Elvis was laid in a steel-lined copper coffin, flown in from Oklahoma City. He wore a white suit from Lansky brothers that his father had given him and a TCB lightning bolt ring on his finger.

On the day after his death, fans were allowed into Graceland to file past the body. The gates were kept open longer than planned to cope with demand, and they still shut thousands out. Over 200 people needed medical attention that day.

Elvis's cousin Bobby Mann took a photo of Elvis lying in his coffin and sold it for $78,000 to the *National Enquirer*.

The funeral service took place at Graceland on Thursday 18 August. Members of the Memphis Area Broadcasters Association held a minute's silence at 2 p.m. and flags flew at half-mast across the state.

There were 200 guests at the service, and Elvis's favourite quartets were there. Jake Hess sang 'Known Only To Him', and James Blackwood sang 'How Great Thou Art'.

Reverend Bradley of the Wooddale Church of Christ gave the sermon, which included these words: 'From total obscurity Elvis rose to world fame. His name is a household word in every nook and corner of this earth ... Though idolised by millions and forced to be protected from the crowds, Elvis never lost his desire to stay in close touch with humanity ... In a world where so many pressures are brought upon us to lose our identity, to be lost in the masses, Elvis dared to be different. Elvis was different and no one else can ever be exactly like him. Elvis died at forty-two. Some of you may not live to be that old. But it's not how long we live that's really important, but how we live.'

Elvis was taken to Forest Hill Cemetery in a white hearse followed by sixteen white Cadillacs carrying his family and friends. The coffin was strewn with rosebuds, then entombed in a grey marble crypt. The tomb was sealed with concrete and marble.

The superintendent of Forest Hill reckoned that 50,000 people passed through the cemetery gates that day. It had taken a hundred vans to carry all the flowers from Graceland to the cemetery: by the day's end, not a single stem was left.

On 28 August three men attempted to steal Elvis's remains from the tomb at Forest Hill Cemetery. As security concerns showed no signs of abating, the remains of both Elvis and Gladys were moved in October to the Meditation Garden at Graceland.

For years after the funeral, fans would visit the Memphis Funeral Home to see the white hearse that had carried Elvis's body. After the bonnet ornament had been stolen several times, the managers finally gave up and left the bonnet bare.

'Elvis Presley's death deprives our country of a part of itself; his music and his personality changed the face of American popular culture ... Elvis may be gone but his legend will be with us for a long time to come.' President Jimmy Carter.

'I think it was easier for The Beatles than Elvis ... He was on his own and ... as his life went on, he ended up more and more on his own.' Ringo Starr.

'A lot of us wondered what an old Elvis Presley would be like. Now we will never know. He will always be the King ... and no one can take that away from him.' Pat Boone.

'I wasn't just a fan, I was his brother. Elvis was a hard worker, dedicated, and God loved him. I love him and hope to see him in heaven. There'll never be another like that soul brother.' James Brown.

I WANT YOU, I NEED YOU, I LOVE YOU

Elvis was a master at taking a country song and giving it a unique twist. Here are the ten essential country tracks.

'Long Black Limousine', 1969
Available on *From Elvis In Memphis*
Elvis's version of this old tale, of a girl who leaves home to become a star and returns home in a hearse, is filled with passion and anguish and a horrible prophetic poignancy. One of the greatest songs he ever sang.

'I'm Movin' On', 1969
Available on *From Elvis In Memphis*
Elvis starts off country and ends up in a funky soul groove – and all the while he was going down with laryngitis.

'Kentucky Rain', 1969
Available on *From Elvis In Memphis*
This contemporary country song took everybody a few hours to get to grips with but the result is a powerful number that became one of Elvis's show favourites.

'Tomorrow Never Comes', 1970
Available on *Elvis Country*
This builds up and builds up until Elvis nearly explodes. He found it tricky to record and producer Felton Jarvis told him to hang on in there: 'It's gonna be a gas.' Elvis retorted, 'If it ain't, I'm gonna take some.'

'Funny How Time Slips Away', 1970
    Available on *Elvis Country*
    A great, slow, drawling sort of song. While touring Elvis often
    turned up the house lights for this song and at the words,
    'Well, hello there', sent the audience into a frenzy.

'I Washed My Hands In Muddy Water', 1970
    Available on *Elvis Country*
    A tense, hard-driving take on the well-known tale of a man
    going wrong.

'Make The World Go Away', 1970
    Available on *Elvis Country*
    Not surprisingly, Elvis sings this dramatic number as if he
    really, really means it.

'Good Time Charlie's Got The Blues', 1973
    Available on *Promised Land*
    A sad, touching ballad from which, tellingly, Elvis omits the
    lines, 'I take the pills to ease the pain/Can't find a thing to ease
    my brain'.

'There's A Honky Tonk Angel', 1973
    Available on *Promised Land*
    Elvis insisted everyone stayed on to do this because his father
    was visiting the studio and it was Vernon's favourite song. A
    wonderful, classic country number.

'Blue Eyes Crying In The Rain', 1976
    Available on *Moody Blue*
    A beautiful song in its own right, this is forever famous for
    being the last song Elvis ever sang, sitting at the piano in his
    racquetball court in the small hours of 16 August 1977.

I'LL REMEMBER YOU

Like the murder of JFK, Elvis's death is etched in many people's memories, whether they're fans or not. A 2003 Samaritans survey of Britain's most emotional memories places Elvis's death at No. 20, after events such as 9/11, the fall of the Berlin Wall and the first man on the moon.

'I'd been playing in the garden and when I came inside I found my mother sitting on the stairs, crying. I'd never seen her cry before. I asked her what was wrong. She said, "Elvis is dead."'

'I was at a disco which had a revolving floor. The DJ told us Elvis had died and he played Elvis songs the whole night.'

'I was playing Elvis records on my record player and my father came in and said, "I don't know what you're listening to him for. He's dead."'

'I heard it at home in New York. I remember thinking, we'd lost JFK, Bobby Kennedy and Martin Luther King, and I thought, this was another great man gone.'

'I was doing a summer job in a walking-stick factory, putting the rubber bits on the end of the walking sticks. They piped Radio 2 through the factory and I heard it on there. As I recollect it the radio seemed to play nothing much but Elvis for the rest of the summer.'

'I was eleven, in the back seat of our car. My mum was driving, and I've no idea where we were going, but I do remember the radio saying, "The King is dead."'

'I was a young computer programmer when the news came through in the office. Although I'd never been a great fan it was still a shock. The reaction I remember most was a woman co-worker of about thirty who was quite vicious, saying, "He was a disgusting creature, I feel nothing at all about his death."'

'My parents sat me down one morning with very serious looks on their faces. My grandfather, who I didn't know very well, was ill so I assumed they were going to tell me he had died. When they said it was Elvis who had died, I was completely distraught and wished it had been my grandfather . . .'

'When I heard, I'd just bought myself a new car – an Olds Cutlass two-door, blue with a Landau roof. I remember the news as clearly as I remember the car!'

'I heard it on the radio. My friend and I stood there in the kitchen and cried our eyes out.'

'I was working as a lifeguard at an outdoor swimming pool in British Columbia. I was on the deck and another lifeguard, who was a huge Elvis fan, came running out of the guard shack waving his arms, yelling, "Elvis is dead!" I remember the pool, which was very busy, fell really quiet.'

'I was fixing a TV set and listening to Capital Radio late in the evening. I was just wondering why they'd played several Elvis songs in a row when the DJ announced, "The King is dead." All of the pop stations played nothing but Elvis for the rest of the evening.'

'I was living in a bedsit in Preston when I heard it on breakfast radio. I do remember a local TV interview with a man who had collected Elvis memorabilia for years and had so much of it that he had decided it was no longer manageable – so he'd sold it all just a couple of weeks before ...'

'I was working at a bank in Washington. I wasn't particularly bothered about it but one of the women I worked with was crying so much the manager had to call her husband to come and take her home. It was as if she had lost a member of her own family.'

'I was in the spare room with a portable TV, because Mum and Dad were having a dinner party downstairs. I was looking forward to watching *Round The World In 80 Days* but they cancelled it and replaced it with an Elvis concert from Las Vegas – I remember being really annoyed about it! And I couldn't believe how different he looked from his films that I used to watch on Saturday mornings.'

'My wife and I were in the bedroom late in the evening with the radio on when it was announced. We were both absolutely stunned; we couldn't believe it. Elvis was immortal, wasn't he?'

'I was in the shower, listening to Radio 1 when I heard it. And then a while later there was that dreadful song, 'I Remember Elvis Presley'.'

'I was in my room listening to the radio when they announced that the King had passed away. I went immediately to my mother, who is a huge Presley fan, and said, "Hey, Mom. Guess what. Elvis is dead." It was weeks before she stopped wailing.'

'The night before Elvis died, I had watched an old movie of his and dreamed that he had been in a helicopter crash. When I heard the news it was all a bit eerie.'

'I was in the airport in Ibiza. We were going home after our holiday, and a schoolfriend was just arriving to start hers. She told me the news. Her father saw us both sobbing and thought one of our hamsters must have died.'

'We were on holiday in Wales and we'd just come out of an ice-cream parlour when my aunt came up to meet us and told us that Elvis was dead. The family felt really miserable for hours.'

'My son woke me up to tell me the news. I was devastated, not only that he had died but that I hadn't seen him in the flesh, a dream I had cherished since the age of ten. I went to my job as a DJ at a club that evening and we all just sat around exchanging stories and personal takes on Elvis. I didn't eat for days, and played his records wall to wall.'

'My wife and I were driving home from Connecticut when we heard it on the radio. They played Elvis songs all the way back to New York. It was a shock and goes to show how you think someone will be around forever.'

BURNING LOVE

There are fans, and there are Elvis fans. The entries in italics are all items of graffiti from the walls of Graceland.

There are over 600 fan clubs worldwide. The largest is The Official Elvis Presley Fan Club of Great Britain, with over 20,000 members. Next is the French club, called Elvis My Happiness.

Elvis, I wish I was your belt buckle for a day

Father and son Paul and Elvis Aron Presley Macleod, from Holly Springs, Mississippi, claim to be the world's No. 1 Elvis fans. Their house, Graceland Too, is a museum in which every single room is dedicated to Elvis. Paul's wife told him one day to choose between her or his Elvis collection. The Elvis collection won.

Elvis, yesterday I realised how much I love you, so I broke off my engagement

Japan is mad about Elvis. In 2003 Junichiro Koizumi became the country's first Elvis-impersonating Prime Minister. He has released a CD of his favourite Elvis songs and has even sung an Elvis duet with Tom Cruise.

Some people go to Mecca; we go to Graceland for our pilgrimage

Thousands of fans worldwide are members of Meetup. On the first Tuesday of every month, International Elvis Meetup Day, they gather at local venues across the globe to meet other fans and talk about the King.

In the great divide between a life with meaning and one without, there is Graceland

One of the earliest fan publications was *Elvis Presley Speaks!*, published in 1956 and written by a reporter from the *Memphis Press–Scimitar*. In it Elvis reassures his fans, 'I enjoy dating more than anything. Is that wrong?'

Elvis, you still give us 'nguvud na roho' strength of heart – Magic Elvis Club, Kenya

Elvis fan Margie Woods was buried with a cutout of Elvis beside her in the coffin.

My heart stopped on 8-16-77

The world's largest Elvis festival takes place in early August in Collingwood, Ontario, Canada. At Molly Bloom's Irish Pub, thirsty fans can revive themselves with a Hound Dog – a mix of Baileys, Kahlua, Amaretto, Pepsi and milk. Many fans leave this festival and head straight to Memphis for Elvis Week.

Knowing that your door is always open and your path is free to walk keeps you gentle on my mind

A fan from Ireland described a visit to Graceland as 'just like going to see your dad's grave'.

The world is full of beautiful people – Elvis, you are the most beautiful in every way

During Elvis's 1956 visit to New York, Boston DJ Norm Prescott got 5,000 replies to a contest to win hairs plucked from the King's sideburns.

Elvis, you tear the stars from our sky

Elvis gave blood to the German Red Cross in January 1959. Readers of German teen magazine *Bravo* wrote in asking if they could buy some of the Presley blood to inject into their own veins.

Elvis, you're not my first love, but you are my last

Elvis Monthly, the British fan magazine that was distributed worldwide, was first produced by editor Albert Hand when Elvis was in the army. It continued until the late 1990s.

Thank you for your love, your song and your soul

While on the liner *United States* headed for New York, the Duke of Windsor confided to a fellow passenger that the Duchess of Windsor's luggage included most of Elvis's records, and that her favourite Elvis number was 'Hound Dog'.

We are blind without your light

At Audubon Drive, Elvis's home back in 1956, the rule was that fans were welcome to wander around the property provided they weren't disruptive. As a result, fans stole the grass off Elvis's lawn, took cups of water from his tap, and stood with their ears pressed to the wall of his bedroom to hear him snoring. Elvis believed it was his duty never to turn away the fans that had made him.

The days may be crowded, the hours too few, but there is always time for you

By 1956 it took nine secretaries at fan club headquarters to open all of Elvis's fan mail. Elvis joked, 'At least we've given the post-men in Nashville something to do.'

I will live my whole life through loving you

When Elvis visited Jim's Barber Shop in Memphis, girls would come in afterwards looking for bits of his hair to take home. The *Memphis Press–Scimitar* even published an announcement asking girls not to go down there because Elvis never had enough cut off to do anything with. It didn't stop them going, though.

Elvis: America's answer to royalty

After 'Teddy Bear', fans sent Elvis cuddly toys in their thousands. He received 282 bears one Christmas alone.

Elvis has given me more than any soul can give – reach out and he will be there

In 1956, Andrea June Stevens from Atlanta won a competition for a dinner date with Elvis. In her winning essay she described Elvis as 'the brightest star in the entertainment heavens'. She came all the way to Jacksonville to meet him. By the time his show had ended and Elvis was ready to eat, it was past midnight. Then on the way out of the hotel, Elvis stopped to look after a young fan who had just fainted. Andrea's dream date ended up taking place in a cramped diner in the small hours. The press, and Andrea, looked on while Elvis read a newspaper and ate bacon sandwiches.

We wish we could have loved you tender enough to keep you with us

In 1956 *Modern Screen* magazine gave Elvis a 'King of Fan Mail' award for holding the world record for the number of fan letters he received.

Elvis, your burning love left a hole in my heart

In their manifesto for the 2001 general election, the Elvisly Yours Elvis Presley Party made these pledges:

- A sleazeometer in the House of Commons to play 'You ain't nothin' but a hound dog' when an MP registers positive

- Traffic cones to be replaced by pink fluorescent teddy bears

- Britain to remain in Europe provided all MPs wear jump suits in the European Parliament

He touched me and now I am no longer the same

'Elvis had a whole nation in love with him. You may be here because of 'Love Me Tender'.' Ice T.

From a kid to an old man, I will remember

A fan took his small daughter to meet Elvis in Audubon Drive. Elvis kissed her on the cheek, where she had a large birthmark. Whenever people teased her about it, she'd say, 'That's where Elvis kissed me.'

Elvis makes life worth living

The motto of the Mile High on Elvis fan club is 'God Blessed America, He Gave Us Elvis.'

As long as we keep Elvis on our minds, there is a promised land for the future

When Elvis joined the army, he was getting 15,000 fan letters a week.

He is now leading the angelic choir in sweet infinity

In 1996, Indianapolis city planners proposed knocking down their sports complex, Market Square Arena, and building a new one. They were deluged with emotional protests. Market Square Arena was the location of Elvis's final concert. One fan said it would be like tearing down Graceland. The new complex is yet to be realised.

Memories of you are pressed between the pages of my mind

Many fan clubs try to replicate Elvis's generosity. Pittsburgh's 'We Remember Elvis' trains doctors and nurses in the developing world; an Indiana club raises funds for the Special Olympics.

I will embrace him with poetic hands with which to express himself. I will make his voice of cherished velvet, and when he speaks and sings untold beauty and joy will be felt around the world. I will bring his form into the world to bring people together. I will give him riches and love beyond imagination. I will make him unique and irreplaceable in a world of duplication. I will present him to the world as a gift of God, and he will be called ELVIS PRESLEY

WALK A MILE IN MY SHOES

When Elvis died in 1977, there were already several dozen impersonators around the world. There are now tens of thousands of them. If things keep going like this, Elvis impersonators will soon outnumber many small nations. There is certainly no sign of them going out of fashion.

Elvis impersonators are officially known as Elvii.

Top Elvii can earn up to $100,000 a week in Las Vegas.

Famous names include Trent 'The Dream King' Carlini and Max 'Elvis to the Max' Pellicano. Noted British impersonators include Louis Rockafella, Steve Preston and Liberty Mounten. One of Australia's leading impersonators is Eddie Youngblood.

Other notable Elvii include the lesbian Elvis Herselvis, Bearded Elvis, Physicist Elvis and Nude Elvis. Green Elvis performs environmentally friendly versions of the King's hits; thus 'Don't Be Cruel' becomes 'Don't Waste Fuel'.

The Mexican El-Vez has brought out CDs entitled *Graciasland* and *GI Ay Ay! Blues*. He is so highly thought of that he has his own impersonator.

The two biggest impersonator contests every year are at the Elvis festival in Collingwood, Ontario, and the Images of the King contest, which climaxes in Memphis during Elvis Week.

Elvii spend hours practising Elvis moves for their performance. Gestures include the lasso, the body palsy, glass on palm and the backhanded throwaway.

The Flying Elvii are a team of ten white-jumpsuited skydivers who featured in the Nicolas Cage film *Honeymoon In Vegas*. They earn a fortune jumping from 10,000 feet to open shopping malls and launch products such as the Viva Las Vegas credit card.

Many of Elvis's backing musicians, including Scotty Moore, D.J. Fontana, the Jordanaires and the Sweet Inspirations, have also backed Elvii.

Impersonators flock to get their outfits from B&K Enterprises of Charlestown, Indiana. The company did the jump suits for the film *3,000 Miles To Graceland* and will provide the whole she-bang for you, including capes for around $1,500 and belts for about $300. Remember, the embroidered suits are dry clean only; tell the cleaner to use 'a short cycle, with low moisture'.

A top-quality Elvis wig, custom made out of human hair, can cost $1,000.

At the Graceland Wedding Chapel in Las Vegas, an Elvis imper-sonator will serenade you, act as best man, or give the bride away – but sorry, he can't marry you.

Paul 'The Wonder Of' Hyu is Britain's leading Chinese Elvis and the self-proclaimed 'King of Wok'n'Roll'. He had a starring role in the video for JXL's remix of 'A Little Less Conversation', and is the only Chinese Elvis registered with the actors' union Equity.

In October 2003 a Norwegian Elvis impersonator regained a world record by singing Elvis songs for over forty hours. Kjell Henning Bjoernestad, better known as Kjell Elvis, sang 786 songs in forty hours, eight minutes and one second – the eight and one symbolised Elvis's birthday, 8 January.

South Africa's Elvis Impersonator contest for 2003 was held at the Carnival City Casino. The 20,000 rand first prize went to Lionel Hunt. Runner-up was Fanie Schoeman, who has loved Elvis since childhood and has spoken in a Tennessee drawl since the age of twelve, despite speaking Afrikaans and living on a sheep farm.

An Elvisoid is someone who dresses up as Elvis but doesn't perform. Kansas City has an annual Elvisoid parade with thousands of participants.

Europe's largest Elvis convention took place in January 2004, in Blackpool. The name of the event was, of course, 'Walk a Golden Mile in my shoes'. Matt King of Surbiton won the professional contest, beating Vladimir Lichnovsky of the Czech Republic into second place. A Black Elvis head-to-head contest between Britain's Colbert Hamilton and America's Bibby Simmons was declared a draw.

Bibby Simmons' website announces simply: 'He is back. This time he is black.'

Impersonators perform for free every day at the Elvis-A-Rama memorabilia museum in Las Vegas. You can also see Elvis's very own blue suede shoes between shows.

Dennis Wise was a car salesman from Hawaii who had plastic surgery so he could fulfil his dream of becoming an Elvis impersonator.

The annual Elvis festival in Parkes, New South Wales, has soundalike *and* lookalike contests.

In 2002, impersonator Mark W. Curran from Los Angeles spent thirty days on Route 66 in an Elvis Across America Roadathon to promote heritage sites along the route.

Johnny Thompson founded the Professional Elvis Impersonators Association (PEIA) in 2001. Its aim is 'the advancement of Elvis Presley's music and style throughout the world'. Among its code of ethics is: 'I have an obligation as an Elvis Impersonator in all my personal, business and social contacts, to be conscious of my image and what I represent and to conduct myself accordingly.'

In 1977 Elvis wrote to an impersonator, David Ferrari, to congratulate him on winning a talent competition. He added, 'Do develop your own special talents, though . . . never neglect your own special abilities to be yourself also.'

RETURN TO SENDER

It seems that for Elvis Presley, philately really will get you everywhere.

Nobody but British royalty has appeared on the stamps of more countries than Elvis.

Among the nations who have honoured Elvis on their stamps are Germany, Gambia, Tanzania, Grenada, Dominica, Antigua and the Maldives.

Elvis was the first rock'n'roll artist ever to grace a US stamp. Many people were against the idea because of his less than saintly lifestyle. But as Postmaster General Anthony Frank said, 'He won't be the first flawed American to show up on a stamp.'

The American Civil Liberties Union announced that an Elvis stamp would be unconstitutional. Putting the King on a stamp would violate the article that states, 'No title of nobility shall be granted by the United States.' It's not entirely clear if they were joking . . .

The American public was asked to choose which of two images of Elvis would be on the stamp – 1950s Elvis, or 1970s Elvis. The images were unveiled at a ceremony in Las Vegas, where Anthony Frank joked, 'Younger Elvis would be fifty stamps to a sheet. Older Elvis would be forty.' Over 1.2 million people voted, and skinny Elvis won.

The stamp was officially released for sale on 8 January 1993, which would have been Elvis's 58th birthday. It was the most successful commemorative release in the US Postal Service's history, and net profit exceeded $25 million.

Hundreds of Elvis fans sent letters with Elvis stamps to imaginary addresses, in order to have the letters returned bearing the legend, 'Return to sender, address unknown.'

In 1993 a female fan with throat cancer claimed to be miraculously cured after licking an Elvis commemorative stamp.

I want you, I need you, I love you

'I get carried away very easily. Emotional sonofabitch,' confessed Elvis. Which is why he sang about love like nobody else. Here are the ten essential Elvis ballads.

'Love Me', 1956

Available on *The King Of Rock'n'Roll: The Complete 50s Masters*

Leiber and Stoller wrote this as a spoof, but Elvis sings it straight and defies anyone *not* to love him by the end of it. One of Elvis's own favourites.

'Don't', 1957

Available on *The King Of Rock'n'Roll*

This is a fabulous ballad, written especially for Elvis, who gets the balance between mournful pleading and horniness just right. D.J. Fontana's – and Paul Gambaccini's – favourite Elvis song.

'Are You Lonesome Tonight', 1960

Available on *Elvis Is Back*

Elvis recorded this as a favour to Colonel Parker's wife. He sang it with the lights down low, and the spoken part is a fine dramatic performance. This is Boris Yeltsin's all-time top song, apparently. The Laughing Version, from a 1969 live show, is a hit among fans, including Terry Wogan who says it's his favourite Elvis number.

'Suppose', 1966
   Available on *The Home Recordings*
   This is Elvis just singing for pleasure at home in Graceland, with Charlie Hodge at the piano, captured on Red West's tape recorder. It is simply a very beautiful song.

'In The Ghetto', 1969
   Available on *From Elvis In Memphis*
   Not many millionaire superstars could sing this song and get away with it, but Elvis sings it with incredible sensitivity and dignity. The familiarity of this song never diminishes its power.

'How The Web Was Woven', 1970
   Available on *That's The Way It Is*
   Superb vocal control takes Elvis through this soulful number in one long, beautifully executed lament.

'Just Pretend', 1970
   Available on *That's The Way It Is*
   A gorgeous love song that Elvis just pours his heart into.

'Always On My Mind', 1972
   Available on *Burning Love*
   Elvis's personal reflections on his marriage seem to come painfully to the fore in a lovely and rightfully lauded hit song. This is Boy George's favourite song.

'Loving Arms', 1973
   Available on *Promised Land*
   A perfect Elvis ballad. He practically calls out in pain in the second verse – laying it all bare for his audience, as ever.

'Hurt', 1976

Available on *Moody Blue*

Elvis sings 'I'm so hurt' with such pain and sincerity, it's no wonder the critic Greil Marcus called this song 'apocalyptic'. Late Presley at his best.

ALWAYS ON MY MIND

Elvis may be dead (or maybe not) but he is still very much alive in our popular culture and modern mythology. His name is a one-word code that the whole world can decipher.

'No matter what you do, you can not, not, not, not mess up for Elvis, or change anything, 'cause you'll change history. Big time.' Al to Sam (as Elvis) in *Quantum Leap*.

In just four months after Elvis's death, over 200 records about him were released worldwide; in 1978, there were 100 more.

Elvis The Musical opened at the Astoria Theatre in London in 1978. It starred two unknowns called Shakin' Stevens and Tracey Ullman.

Quentin Tarantino has quite an Elvis thing going on. In *Pulp Fiction*, Uma Thurman's character observes that you're either an Elvis person or a Beatles person, and some Tarantino fans are convinced that Marsellus's suitcase contains Elvis's gold suit. Meanwhile, Buck, the nurse from *Kill Bill*, sports a stylish pair of Elvis sunglasses.

In the film *Mighty Joe Young*, the eponymous gorilla is secretly transported to an American wildlife park. A park worker signals his safe arrival by announcing into her walkie-talkie, 'Elvis is in the building.'

Elvis's name has appeared in many book titles, including *Elvis Is Dead And I'm Not Feeling So Good Myself* by humorist Lewis Grizzard, and *Lose Weight Through Great Sex With Celebrities The Elvis Way* by Colin MacEnroe.

A commemorative Elvis plate hangs on the living-room wall of the Conner's home in the US sitcom *Roseanne*.

A British TV ad for KitKat chocolate featured a jumpsuited Elvis hiding out in a northern fish and chip shop. The tag line? 'Take a break', of course.

In Gary Panter's comic book *Invasion Of The Elvis Zombies*, Elvis is eaten by his female fans and is brought back to life as a hybrid of himself, King Kong and Godzilla.

Nicolas Cage is an Elvis obsessive who won himself the ultimate piece of memorabilia when he married Lisa Marie. He has appeared in two Elvis-related movies: *Honeymoon In Vegas*, with its '34 Flying Elvises, Utah Chapter', and the David Lynch road movie *Wild At Heart*, where Cage beats someone up then softly sings 'Love Me Tender'.

The Far Side cartoonist Gary Larson once drew Elvis and Salman Rushdie peering out at the world through the window blinds of their shared apartment.

In 1990 a tribute album was issued in aid of a music charity. *The Last Temptation Of Elvis* included Paul McCartney singing 'It's Now Or Never', Bruce Springsteen singing 'Viva Las Vegas', and the Pogues singing 'Got A Lot O' Livin' To Do'.

In 1988 the US *Sun* reported that a statue of Elvis had been found on Mars, and a radio receiver was picking up strains of 'All Shook Up'. Ufologist Nikola Stanislaw concluded that aliens must have built it believing Elvis to be some sort of god. This was the only rational explanation.

Elvis has been the muse for countless artists, most famously in Andy Warhol's series of silk-screened lithographs. Another artist, Gunter Blum, depicted the Statue of Liberty holding up a guitar instead of a torch, with a photo of Elvis in her other hand and a definite lip curl.

In *The Cosby Show*, Grandfather Huxtable ponders, 'Crazy world – hasn't been the same since Elvis and Priscilla broke up.'

At a temple in a small town in the Indian state of Karnataka, a picture of Elvis hangs beside the usual images of Hindu gods. The temple is attached to the home of a man who published a booklet in Elvis's name, entitled *Why My Daughter Married Michael Jackson*.

The Cartoon Network's Johnny Bravo is a bequiffed Elvis soundalike who does karate and lives with his mum.

When British protesters against the 2003 Iraq war were demonstrating against the Defence Secretary Geoff Hoon, one of their placards exclaimed, 'You ain't nothing but a Hoon dog lying all the time.'

In *The X-Files*, Fox Mulder refers to a closed-minded agent as 'the type of person who thinks Elvis is dead'. In one particular episode Mulder uses vacation time for what he tells Scully is a 'spiritual journey' – he never tells her he's headed for Graceland.

A tyre ad for a trade magazine showed a picture of Elvis with the line 'Only Elvis has as many fans . . . If you think Elvis is a mover, stock Pirelli. You'll be worked off your blue suede shoes.'

In Douglas Adams' *Mostly Harmless*, the first thing we discover about the recently landed aliens is that they have a liking for Elvis Presley and are monitoring with interest the theory that he was captured by (other) aliens.

On the New York stage, Christopher Walken wrote and starred in *Him*, in which Elvis mooched around in limbo, haunted by lookalikes, on his way to the next life.

Bill Clinton's flamboyant presidential inauguration in 1993 included in its parade a float full of impersonators under the banner 'Elvis is alive'. Clinton sang 'Don't Be Cruel' in an interview in response to allegations about his personal life. And his aides referred to their sleepless world as 'Elvis time', due to Clinton's round-the-clock work schedule.

George Bush Sr described Clinton's recovery plan as 'Elvis economics' that would lead to 'Heartbreak Hotel'. This backfired as commentators pointed out that more people tuned in to watch Elvis singing 'Heartbreak Hotel' than tuned in to watch the Republican convention, and Elvis was still earning a fortune without doing anything. As *USA Today* said, 'Now *that's* a record you can run on.'

Elvissey, by Jack Womack, is a novel set in 2033, when people worship every Sunday at the C of E – the Church of Elvis. A big corporation sends an operative back to 1954 to retrieve the King for his fans, but when she gets there she finds Elvis standing over the blood-spattered body of his mother . . .

Following TV wit David Letterman's suggestion, US baseball commentators took to announcing 'Elvis has left the building' whenever anyone got a home run.

In *Independence Day*, as the aliens draw near, a woman moans, 'Oh God, I hope they bring back Elvis.'

The first International Conference on Elvis Presley took place in August 1995 at the University of Mississippi. Lecture themes included 'Elvis Presley and the White Acquiescence of Black Rhythms' and 'Dead Elvis as Other Jesus'.

Carla, the feisty barmaid in *Cheers*, hopes that new management will enable her to have a proper holiday – six weeks at Graceland instead of the usual one.

In his hit song 'Without Me', Eminem tells how he's seen as the worst thing since Elvis Presley, while a white-suited impersonator boogies round the bathroom in the accompanying video.

When *Rolling Stone* magazine featured Jerry Seinfeld, he was described as The King (of Comedy), and there were two different cover shots for the issue: Seinfeld wore gold lamé on one, and a jump suit on the other.

Sonny Crockett's pet alligator on *Miami Vice* was called Elvis.

A 1996 *USA Today* advert for *The Lion King* postage stamps proclaimed: 'Move over Elvis . . . Collectors Proclaim Simba the New King.'

In 2003 the *Steve Wright Show* on Radio 2 introduced 'Ask Elvis', where a soundalike discussed everyday dilemmas such as how to train a cat to use a cat flap, and getting the best from a Yorkshire pudding.

In *The Frighteners*, an Elvis statue floats through a house possessed by poltergeists. The homeowner cries, 'He's alive!'

Elvis became the first person ever to feature on plastic when Leader Federal Savings and Loan of Memphis issued an Elvis Mastercard in 1988. The response was three times higher than a normal credit card ad provoked.

When Jim Carrey transforms from zero to hero in *The Mask*, he spins through a selection of famous characters, including Elvis mumbling, 'Thank you very much'.

When Merrick approaches the eponymous Buffy to recruit her to a life of vampire slaying, she asks sarcastically, 'Does Elvis talk to you? Does he tell you to do things?'

In *Flatliners*, a group of medics uses dangerous experiments to sample the afterlife. When they boast to a café waitress, 'We just came back from the dead!' she shrugs and replies, 'I'm not surprised. We had Elvis in here last night.'

During Britain's 1992 parliamentary campaign, a psychic reported for the *Sun* that while Josef Stalin and John Lennon were on the side of Neil Kinnock, Winston Churchill and Elvis were rooting for John Major.

Mad magazine once predicted that the most popular names for boys in the future would be Elvis and Frankenstein.

In *Forrest Gump*, Elvis comes to stay at the Gumps' boarding house and the eponymous hero teaches him his leg-shake.

Rosie Nieper T-shirts Ltd sells a marvellous garment for the conspiracy theorists among us, emblazoned with the words, 'Nobody knows I'm Elvis'.

In *The Commitments* there's a portrait of Elvis on the wall, beside those of the Pope and the Virgin Mary, in the Rabbitte household.

Paul Simon stars as a failing folk singer in *One-Trick Pony*. His exasperated wife tells him, 'You have wanted to be Elvis Presley since you were thirteen. Now that's a goal you're not likely to achieve. He didn't do so well with it himself.'

The Client features, in passing, an Elvis Pez candy dispenser.

Pete Postlethwaite describes a parasaurolophus dinosaur as 'the one with the big red horn – the pompadour-Elvis' in *Jurassic Park: The Lost World*.

A character in *Con Air* says, 'If that aircraft's carrying thirty prisoners, then I'm Elvis Presley.' When the plane later lands on the Vegas strip, Nicolas Cage says, 'Well, Viva Las Vegas.'

An 80s ad for Memorex tape – with the slogan 'Is it real or is it Memorex?' – featured top Elvis impersonator Clayton Mark. Mark broke a glass singing what appeared to be 'American Trilogy' but which for copyright reasons was actually part of 'John Brown's Body'.

In *Men In Black*, when Tommy Lee Jones puts Elvis on the car stereo, Will Smith says, 'You do know Elvis is dead, right?' Jones replies, 'No, Elvis is not dead – he just went home.'

In 2003 *The Weakest Link* quiz show did an Elvis special, in which all the contestants were Elvis impersonators.

Talking about his former ruinous spending habits, actor-turned-boxer Mickey Rourke recently described himself as being like Elvis on acid.

Where would the spectacular musical *Joseph And The Amazing Technicolor Dreamcoat* have been without its bequiffed, 'uh-huh'ing Pharaoh?

Demi Moore has a picture of Elvis on her wall in *Striptease*.

Jailhouse Rock: The Musical premiered at the Plymouth Theatre Royal in February 2004. Elvis's cousin Donna Presley Early came to Plymouth to promote the show.

The Simpsons is heaving with Elvis references: when Homer becomes a music manager, he gets a suit made from material 'specially designed for Elvis – sweat actually cleans it'; a photo of Elvis taken with Mr Burns exactly replicates the famous Presley–Nixon image; one of Bart's detention lines is 'I did not see Elvis'.

Recent movie *Bubba Ho-Tep* (2002) pairs up an aged Elvis with a guy who thinks he's JFK to fight an evil mummy. Bruce Campbell, who plays Elvis, told *Empire* magazine that once the make-up was on, it was easy to do Elvis – you just have to wander around and mumble.

All Shook Up, a musical inspired by and featuring the songs of Elvis, is due to hit Broadway in spring 2005.

Kirsty MacColl didn't believe the guy down the chip shop who swore he was Elvis – but there are plenty of people who would. At www.elvissightingbulletinboard.com we are kept informed of Presley's whereabouts. The bulletin board 'is offered as a public service so that the public will not be alarmed when seeing The King at their local supermarket or skinny-dipping in the neighbour's pool. Imagine it, you go to the supermarket in curlers and there, next to you in line, is The King!'

Kalamazoo, Michigan, is the Elvis-sighting capital of the world.

William Hill is offering odds of 1000–1 that Elvis will be found alive in 2004.

RAGS TO RICHES

From virtual bankruptcy in 1977, Elvis's estate now makes over $100 million a year.

In his lifetime, Elvis generated revenues of almost four billion dollars. Yet when he died he left an estate worth just $7 million. Everything he owned was visible – Graceland, cars, homes in LA. He didn't even have a pension fund.

Graceland was costing half a million dollars a year to run, most of which went on security. The Internal Revenue Service was demanding millions in death duties. There was no money coming in from song royalties (see 'Big Boss Man'). It was possible that Graceland would have to be sold.

When Vernon died in 1979, Priscilla Presley was among the executors of his will. She set about forming Elvis Presley Enterprises (EPE), named after the original EPE that Colonel Parker had created back in the 1950s. The first thing she did was spend half a million dollars refurbishing Graceland to be more as she remembered it – in other words, removing most of Linda Thompson's décor. She opened it to the public in 1982 and recouped her money in forty days.

Right from the day of Elvis's funeral, enterprising types had been selling everything from memorial T-shirts to phials of Graceland earth, right under the noses of the Presleys. Lawyer Roger

193

Richman drew up a bill that became known as the Tennessee Celebrity Rights Law, passed in 1983. This retrospectively granted that the rights and image of any star would automatically pass to that person's heirs. EPE was about to gain control of the Elvis merchandising industry.

The first thing EPE copyrighted was the epitaph on Elvis's grave.

Fans write in daily with ideas for Elvis merchandise. Most ideas are rejected on the grounds of taste, including one proposal to convert the Circle G ranch into a cemetery for Elvis fans. If EPE approves an idea, strict quality-control rules are applied. For example, no licensee is allowed to use a picture of Elvis looking overweight.

With the power, came the paranoia. EPE really doesn't want anybody else to have anything to do with Elvis. They stopped the production of a ballet about Elvis by the Peter Schauffuss Ballet Company of Denmark. They tried to make it illegal to be an Elvis impersonator. They even tried to copyright 'Thankyouverymuch'. Today, after a lot of court battles and extreme unpleasantness, the use of Elvis's name and image in books and films is protected under freedom-of-speech legislation.

EPE's number one enemy is Sid Shaw, a British fan and owner of Elvisly Yours. Elvisly Yours won a landmark legal battle against EPE and is now legally permitted to supply Elvis merchandise to all of the world – except the USA. You can visit Elvisly Yours in the flesh at 233 Baker Street, London, or at www.elvisly-yours.com.

EPE's heavy-handedness infuriates Sid Shaw. In his essay titled 'DisGraceland', delivered to the Elvis Symposium 2003–04, he writes, 'I know of no business anywhere in the world that so alienates nearly all people associated with that business ... EPE are the complete antithesis to Elvis.'

EPE has nonetheless recognised a need to reflect something of Elvis's outlook on life. It formed the Elvis Presley Charitable Foundation and now supports numerous charities, just as Elvis did.

What'd I Say?

From startled new sensation to jaded living legend, here, in his own words and in strict chronological order, is what the King thought of it all.

'When my first record came out it was a little eerie, I mean . . . I thought people would laugh.'

On Colonel Parker: 'I don't know for sure . . . I don't think I'd have ever been very big if it wasn't for him. He's a very smart man.'

On clothes: 'I like 'em as flashy as you can get 'em.'

'All my life, I've always had a pretty nice time. We didn't have any money or nothing, but I always managed.'

'It all happened so fast till . . . I'm afraid to wake up, afraid it's liable to be a dream . . . afraid I might be back driving a truck again.'

'My Daddy's got Presley's Used Car Lot out on Audubon Drive. I do have four Cadillacs. I haven't got any use for four, I just, ah, maybe someday I'll go broke and I can sell a couple of 'em.'

'I never written a song in my life. I wish I could . . . But me, I did good to get out of high school.'

'I enjoy rock'n'roll. As long as it lasts, as long as it sells, I'll continue doing it, as long as that's what people want. And if they change, if it dies out, I'll try to do something else, and if that doesn't work, I'll just say, well, I had my day.'

'I don't like to be called Elvis the Pelvis, it's one of the most childish expressions I've ever heard. Elvis the Pelvis. But if they wanna call me that there's nothing I can do about it.'

'The very first appearance after I started recording . . . I came out and I was doing a fast-type tune and everybody was hollering and I didn't know what they were hollering at. Then I came off stage and my manager told me they was hollering because I was wiggling my legs. And I was unaware of what I was doing . . . So I went back out for an encore and I did a little more. And the more I did, the wilder they went.'

'I've never turned down a reporter. I've never turned down a disc jockey. I have never been sassy to one. In fact, I've never been sassy to anyone.'

'I sing the way I do, and act the way I do, because it comes natural to me while I'm singing. I wouldn't do it if I thought it wasn't the right thing to do, or if I thought someone was being hurt by it. If I thought that, I'd pack up and go back home and never sing another note.'

'I've been kind of nervous all my life . . . They say you learn how to relax when you get older. I hope they're right.'

On his screen test: 'People shout "Quiet!" and then all of a sudden you're supposed to be acting a part. It's enough to make your legs slide out from under you. Whenever I get excited I

197

stutter a little bit. I have a hard time saying any words that start with W or I. Well I can tell you I really had a hard time with the Ws and Is that day.'

'I like the piano, though I guess I don't play it the way you're supposed to. I just hit whatever keys look good to me.'

'Music tells me more than anything else I've ever known, how good, how great it is just to be alive.'

'I get such a thrill out of [performing] till I wear myself out. Sometimes we have three or four shows a day and it's the same thing as a fighter going into the ring three times in one night. And not many fighters will do it.'

'I always go out with the thought in my mind, "Are they gonna like me, or are they gonna throw rocks at me?"'

'Some people tap their feet. Some people snap their fingers. And some people just sway back and forth. I just sort of do 'em all together I guess.'

When asked whom he tries to appeal to: 'Honey, I'd appeal to the apes in Africa if I could.'

On the Million Dollar Quartet: 'I hate to get started in these jam sessions. I'm always the last one to leave, always.'

'I hope I can continue to record good songs and everything. After all, the minute I stop pleasing them, I'm dead.'

'Regardless of what you do, there're gonna be people that don't like you. There was only one perfect man and that was Jesus

Christ, and people didn't like him . . . I mean, if everybody liked the same thing, we'd all be driving the same car and married to the same woman and it wouldn't work out.'

'I know practically every religious song that's ever been written.'

'I can take ridicule and slander and I've been called names right to my face. That I can take. But I've had a few guys that tried to take a swing at me and naturally you can't just stand there. You have to do something.'

When asked what happens if rock'n'roll dies out while he's in the army: 'I'll starve to death, sir.'

'In Fort Hood . . . I was sitting down on my foot locker and my left leg was shaking. I mean just unconsciously. [The sergeant] said, "Presley, I wish you'd quit shaking that leg." I said, "Sarge, when that leg quits shaking I'm finished."'

'I've tried to play it straight in the army. It's the only way it could be. I couldn't be or do except just what the other boys do. And I'm glad that it turned out the way it has because I've made a lot of friends that I would have never made before.'

On his return from the army: 'Someone asked me this morning, what did I miss about Memphis, and I said, "Everything".'

'I've tried to be the same all through this thing . . . And I always considered other people's feelings. I didn't kick anybody on the way.'

'I have blood running through my veins, and can be snuffed out in just a matter of seconds.'

'Funny, [my mother] never really wanted anything, you know, anything fancy. She just stayed the same, all the way through the whole thing. I wish . . . there's a lot of things happened since she passed away that I wish she could have been around to see. It would have made her very happy and very proud. But that's life and I can't . . . can't have her.'

'When I am pushed to a certain point, I have a very bad temper, an extremely bad temper. So much to the point I have no idea what I'm doing. And then I don't like myself later.'

On films: 'I'd like to do something someday where I feel that I've really done a good job . . . But, in the meantime, if I can entertain people with the things I'm doing, well I'd be a fool to tamper with it . . . If you goof a few times, you don't get many more chances in this business. That's the sad part about it.'

'I certainly haven't lost my respect for my fans. I withdraw not from my fans, but from myself.'

In the 1968 TV special: 'Wait a minute. There's something wrong with my lip. [Curls lip.] You remember that, don't ya? I got news for you, baby, I did 29 pictures like that.'

While on stage: 'You have to drink a lot of water during these shows . . . So if I stop, just watch me . . . "Is that him? I thought he was bigger than that. Hair flying everywhere, he's gotta be a weirdo, man. Stone cold natural freak."'

While on stage: 'MGM is doing a movie here, so don't let these cameras throw you, and try not to throw the cameras. Those of you who have never seen me before will realise tonight that I'm totally insane, and have been for a number of years. They just haven't caught me yet.'

In 1971, when he was honoured by the Jaycees (Junior Chamber of Commerce) as one of America's Ten Outstanding Young Men of the Year: 'When I was a child, ladies and gentlemen, I was a dreamer. I read comic books and I was the hero of the comic book. I saw movies and I was the hero in the movie. So every dream that I ever dreamed has come true a hundred times. And these gentlemen over here, you see these type of people who care, that are dedicated. You realise that it's not [im]possible that they might be building the kingdom of heaven. It's not too far-fetched from reality. I'd like to say that I learned very early in life that without a song, the day would never end. Without a song, a man ain't got a friend. Without a song, the road would never bend, without a song. So I'll keep singing a song. Good night.'

'My dad had seen a lot of people who'd played guitar and stuff, who didn't work. So he said, "Make up your mind about either being an electrician or playing a guitar. I never saw a guitar player that was worth a damn."'

'I've never gotten over what they call stage fright . . . I never get completely comfortable with [the show]. It's a new audience and they haven't seen us before, so it's gotta be like the first time we go on.'

'I think there's room for everybody. I hate to criticise another performer.'

'The image is one thing, and a human being is another. It's very hard to live up to an image.'

When asked about war protests: 'I'd just as soon keep my own personal views about that to myself. 'Cause I'm just an entertainer and I'd rather not say.'

'If nobody recognised me or asked for an autograph . . . I think I would miss it.'

The remaining quotes all come from live performances

'I'd like to praise my orchestra and backup group. I change songs and switch around . . . they never miss a lick. The guys using sheet music have heart failure, but they always catch up with me.'

'I call [the Sweet Inspirations] my analysts. If anything goes wrong I go in their dressing room and I close the door and I confess everything to 'em.'

When a stuffed gorilla is thrown on stage: 'Don't you move, you big sonofabitch. I told the Colonel to stay off the stage!'

'You know that thing about hell hath no fury like a woman scorned, that's so true. I mean, they got the power of the devil himself. Oh Lord, I love 'em, you can't live without 'em.'

In 1974: 'We're gonna sing a lot of songs and try to make you happy. Make you forget about Watergate and all that jazz.'

'When I got sick . . . I heard I was strung out on heroin . . . If I find the individual that has said that about me . . . I will pull your goddamn tongue out by the roots! Thank you very much.'

'You want a scarf? Who do you think I am, the Pope?'

To security staff: 'Don't be so rough on the people when they come down here. Don't treat 'em like they're going to jail, goddammit.'

'I was at a football game and a lady asked a friend of mine, "I hear Elvis Presley's here." My friend said, "Yeah." She said, "I hear he's in the bathroom." He said, "Yeah?" The lady said, very seriously, "I didn't think he did that."'

'[Comedian] Mort Sahl said that Elvis Presley was truly one of the nicest people in the world. And I wish I could agree with him.'

When a fan screams at him to take his suit off: 'Take it off? Are you kidding? It took me two hours to get into it.'

'We're here to entertain you and make you happy . . . till we meet again, may God bless you. Adios.'

FUNNY HOW TIME SLIPS AWAY

Elvis is so omnipresent he seems to exist outside time, but of course he had his era, just like the rest of us. Here's a rundown of Elvis's life, year by year, and some notable moments from the world he inhabited.

1935

Elvis is born on 8 January in Tupelo, Mississippi.

Greta Garbo stars in *Anna Karenina*.

1936

Elvis survives a tornado that sweeps through Tupelo, killing 235.

Jesse Owens wins four gold medals at the Berlin Olympics.

1937

Elvis becomes a regular at the newly built First Assembly of God church near his home.

Amelia Earhart disappears during a flight across the Pacific Ocean.

1938

Vernon Presley begins nine months in prison for forging a cheque.

The radio broadcast of H.G. Wells' *War Of The Worlds* causes panic.

1939

Elvis and Gladys move out of his birthplace for financial reasons, never to return.

World War II begins.

1940

The Presleys move to Maple Street, East Tupelo.

Ernest Hemingway's *For Whom The Bell Tolls* is published.

1941

Elvis enters first grade at the East Tupelo Consolidated School.

Joe DiMaggio hits safely in 56 consecutive games, establishing a major league record.

1942

Vernon's financial worries ease temporarily as he finds work as a carpenter.

Enrico Fermi splits the atom.

1943

Elvis lives for a month on the Gulf Coast while Vernon works in Pascagoula.

Jackson Pollock has his first one-man show.

1944

Vernon keeps the same job all year and the Presleys breathe easy.

Tennessee Williams' *The Glass Menagerie* is published.

1945

Elvis sings 'Old Shep' in a talent contest, and comes fifth.

World War II ends.

1946

Elvis is given a guitar for his birthday.

The US navy tests an atomic bomb at Bikini Atoll.

1947

Grandmother Minnie Mae moves in with Elvis after her marriage breaks up, and remains with him ever afterwards.

Maria Callas makes her debut in *Gioconda*.

1948

The Presleys move to Memphis.

Gandhi is assassinated.

1949

Elvis starts at Humes High School.

Orson Welles stars in *The Third Man*.

1950

Elvis starts work as an usher at the Loew's State cinema in Memphis.

Senator Joseph McCarthy begins his communist witch-hunt.

1951

Elvis passes his driving test.

J.D. Salinger's *The Catcher In The Rye* is published.

1952

Vernon buys Elvis his first car, a 1941 Lincoln.

Elizabeth II succeeds to the throne.

1953

Elvis graduates from high school.

Hillary and Tenzing climb Mount Everest.

1954

'That's All Right' is released.

Roger Bannister runs a mile in 3 minutes 59.4 seconds.

1955

Elvis signs with Colonel Parker and RCA.

Rosa Parks refuses to give up her seat to a white passenger on an Alabama bus, thus becoming an icon of the civil rights movement.

1956

Elvis goes to Hollywood.

Grace Kelly marries Prince Rainier of Monaco.

1957

Elvis buys Graceland.

Dr Seuss's *The Cat In The Hat* is published.

1958

Elvis enters the army.

NASA is established.

1959

Elvis meets Priscilla Beaulieu.

Fidel Castro becomes premier of Cuba.

1960

Elvis returns to civilian life.

Alfred Hitchcock's *Psycho* is released.

1961

Elvis gives his last live performance for seven years.

Yuri Gagarin orbits the earth.

1962

Elvis buys a Dodge motor home for his trips between LA and Memphis.

Marilyn Monroe dies.

1963

Priscilla moves into Graceland.

Lee Harvey Oswald assassinates President Kennedy.

1964

Elvis is appointed Special Deputy Sheriff of Shelby County.

Cassius Clay wins the world heavyweight boxing championship.

1965

Elvis becomes involved with the Self-Realization Fellowship.

The Sound Of Music is released.

1966

Elvis works with one of his favourite producers, Felton Jarvis, for the first time.

Quotations Of Chairman Mao is a bestseller.

1967

Elvis marries Priscilla in Las Vegas.

Twiggy takes America by storm.

1968

Lisa Marie is born. Elvis makes his TV comeback.

Martin Luther King is assassinated in Memphis.

1969

Elvis makes his triumphant return to Vegas.

Neil Armstrong and Buzz Aldrin walk on the moon.

1970

Elvis pays a visit to President Nixon.

John Wayne stars in *True Grit*.

1971

The Junior Chamber of Commerce names Elvis one of the Ten Outstanding Men of the Year.

Sylvia Plath's *The Bell Jar* is published.

1972

Elvis plays New York.

Marlon Brando stars in *The Godfather*.

1973

Elvis performs his televised Hawaii concert, and divorces Priscilla.

Pablo Picasso dies.

1974

Elvis establishes the Tennessee Karate Institute.

President Nixon resigns over Watergate.

1975

Elvis buys aircraft Lisa Marie and Hound Dog II.

Agatha Christie kills off Hercule Poirot in *Curtain.*

1976

Elvis agrees to the widening of Elvis Presley Boulevard in front of Graceland, to ease congestion.

Gymnast Nadia Comaneci gains seven perfect scores at the Montreal Olympics.

1977

Elvis dies on 16 August at Graceland.

Only *Star Wars* can ease the pain.

WHAT NOW MY LOVE

So, you've got the greatest hits album – where does an Elvis
novice go from here? It's a great time to be into Elvis, not least
because RCA/BMG have been remastering albums and adding on
bonus tracks. So, for an overall picture of the King's life and
work, here are the ten essential – and easily available – Elvis
buys.

Last Train To Memphis and Careless Love

This two-part biography by Peter Guralnick (published by
Little, Brown) is the definitive and most level-headed life story
of Elvis. The first part is an exhilarating account of a rise to
superstardom; the second charts a tragic fall of Shakespearean
proportions. You don't need to be an Elvis fan to be enthralled,
and devastated, by this story.

Sunrise

This two-disc compilation CD features all of Elvis's recordings
at Sun Studio. This and *Moody Blue* (see below) perfectly
book-end his extraordinary singing career.

Elvis Presley

Elvis's first album, recorded in 1956, is quite simply a classic,
and a must for anyone who claims to love music. This album
is the essence of how Elvis changed the world.

King Creole

This was Elvis's last film before entering the army, his best, and his favourite. If you're only going to see one Elvis movie (which is probably plenty), then this is the one he'd have wanted you to see.

Elvis Is Back

Elvis came out of the army in 1960 and produced some stunningly good songs with an older, deeper and richer voice. Don't be put off by the appalling cover photo – this album really is superb.

From Elvis In Memphis

This 1969 album came hot on the heels of Elvis's triumphant TV comeback, and is the greatest album of his life. His voice is incredible, his passion tangible. Every home should have this.

That's The Way It Is

Worth the price of a DVD player on its own (or it's on VHS, if you must). This film of rehearsals and 1970 Vegas concerts captures Elvis when he is at his leanest, meanest and keenest. The greatest entertainer who ever lived shows us what he's made of.

Elvis Presley: A Life In Music

Ernst Jorgensen has created a music geek's paradise in this comprehensive chronicle of all of Elvis's recording sessions (published by St Martin's Press). It's almost like being in the studio as Jorgensen brings us the story behind the creation of so many wonderful songs – every note, every comment, every karate kick is wonderfully brought to life.

Moody Blue

The last album of Elvis's lifetime is a love-it-or-hate-it power-house of heartache and regret. Recorded at Graceland in 1976, it's all too easy to imagine the Elvis who sang these songs – a man who had recently told friend and producer Felton Jarvis, 'I'm tired of being Elvis Presley.'

Elvis Fashion: From Memphis To Vegas

This wonderful book by Julie Mundy (published by Universe) is just the thing to cheer you up after *Moody Blue*. It's a glossy celebration of Elvis's style, full of fantastic photos that prove beyond doubt that Elvis was a star, right down to his socks. Gorgeous.

BIBLIOGRAPHY

The information in this book comes from many sources: websites, documentaries, films and albums, tourist boards, fan clubs, and the following books.

Adler, David, *Eating The Elvis Presley Way*, Blake Publishing, 2002.

Bartel, Pauline, *Reel Elvis!*, Taylor Publishing, 1994.

Beaulieu Presley, Priscilla, *Elvis And Me*, Berkley Books, 1985.

Bertrand, Michael T., *Race, Rock And Elvis*, University of Illinois Press, 2000.

Braun, Eric, *The Elvis Film Encyclopedia*, The Overlook Press, 1997.

Chadwick, Vernon, *In Search Of Elvis*, Westview Press, 1997.

Clayton, Rose and Heard, Dick, *Elvis By Those Who Knew Him Best*, Virgin Books, 2002.

Davis Jr, Sammy, *Why Me?*, Michael Joseph, 1989.

Flippo, Chet, *Graceland: The Living Legacy Of Elvis Presley*, Collins, 1993.

Gordon, Robert, *The Elvis Treasures*, Villard, 2002.

Gray, Michael and Osborne, Roger, *The Elvis Atlas*, Henry Holt, 1996.

Grun, Bernard, *The Timetables Of History*, Simon & Schuster, 1991.

Guernsey's, *Elvis: The Official Auction Catalogue*, Harry N. Abrams, 1999.

Guralnick, Peter, *Last Train To Memphis*, Little, Brown, 1994.

Guralnick, Peter, *Careless Love*, Little, Brown, 1999.

Guralnick, Peter and Jorgensen, Ernst, *Elvis Day By Day*, Ballantine Books, 1999.

Hazen, Cindy and Freeman, Mike, *Memphis Elvis-Style*, John F. Blair, 1997.

Humphries, Patrick, *Elvis: The #1 Hits*, Ebury Press, 2002.

Jorgensen, Ernst, *Elvis Presley: A Life In Music*, St Martin's Press, 1998.

Juanico, June, *Elvis: In The Twilight Of Memory*, Warner Books, 1998.

Marcus, Greil, *Mystery Train*, Dutton, 1975.

Marcus, Greil, *Dead Elvis*, Doubleday, 1991.

Mundy, Julie, *Elvis Fashion: From Memphis To Vegas*, Universe Publishing, 2003.

O'Neal, Sean, *Elvis Inc.*, Prima, 1996.

Parker, John, *Elvis: The Secret Files*, Anaya Publishers, 1993.

Plasketes, George, *Images Of Elvis Presley In American Culture*, Harrington Park Press, 1997.

Roberts, David (Ed.), *British Hit Singles, 16th Edition*, Guinness, 2003.

Schröer, Andreas, *Private Presley: The Missing Years*, HarperCollins, 2002.

Simpson, Paul, *The Rough Guide To Elvis*, Rough Guides Ltd, 2002.

Taylor, Roger G., *Elvis In Art*, St Martin's Press, 1987.

Vellenga, Dirk, *Elvis And The Colonel*, Grafton Books, 1990.

Wright, Daniel, *Dear Elvis*, Mustang Publishing, 1996.